Why Men Behave Like APES in Relationships

Keephimattracted.com

This book is designed to provide information and motivation. It is sold with the understanding that the author is not engaged to render any type of psychological, legal, or any other kind of professional advice. Neither the publisher nor the individual author(s) shall be liable for any physical, psychological, emotional, financial, or commercial damages, including, but not limited to, special, incidental, consequential or other damages. You are responsible for your own choices, actions, and results.

Table of Contents

Keephimattracted.com

Intro

It's night, and you're heaving a meal with a great guy. You're on your fourth date. Everything seems fine. He's starting to become your prince charming. You're really happy. But you have this urge. You simply want to ask him, "Where is this going? What do you think about me? What do you think about our future together?" You may want to say, "Why is it you never talk about your emotions or about your feelings? I just wonder."

These are very simple questions. They sound really legitimate. Maybe you even know someone who has asked these questions to a man but was quite disappointed with his response. Maybe the man became more distant; maybe he became silent for the next couple of weeks. His reaction just wasn't what she expected it to be, and you're terrified of that happening to you.

Men are very different than women. If you don't know those differences, it's quite easy to become disappointed because you don't get it. You say, "What did I do?" On the contrary, if you know why a man does what he does, you will have a feeling of power. You'll see why a man does what he does. You'll know it. This knowledge will completely change your relationships with men.

For most women, it's quite hard to find a good man— one that isn't afraid of the "Where is this going?" question. If

Keephimattracted.com

they're lucky enough to find such a man, that guy might eventually begin to do some strange things. He may need his space; he may suddenly slow everything down. He wants to go "fishing" again. As a woman, you want to prevent that from happening. You want to keep your man interested in you and your relationship. And that is exactly what this book is going to show you how to do.

Though English is not my native language, I still find it really important to share my knowledge with you through this book. I've personally been through a lot. However, one way or another I overcame all of my problems. Since I've done that, I've started to help people to overcome their problems as well. In 2008 as a passion project, I started a little website to help men become more successful with women. Pretty soon after that, I had a lot of women emailing me saying, "Hey, why aren't you doing this for us, too?" So I started to really focus on relationships and studied both sexes a lot.

- o Why does a woman pick a certain man?
- o Why does a man fall in love with one woman, but runs away from another?
- o What are the ingredients/laws of attraction?
- o How do you keep the attraction at a very high level, even in a long-term relationship?
- o How do you make sure that even in a long-term relationship neither one wants to find something outside of the relationship and wants to cheat or have an affair?

It has always been my passion to learn and to study why people do what they do. I hope that this book will help you understand why a man does what he does, and how you can create better, deeper, and more fulfilling relationships with men.

Since my first coaching programs where designed for men, I've been surveying men for a long time. I have more than 130,000 men on my mailing list. Quite often I send them a little survey. The results of those surveys are important information for you, as women who want to understand them better.

What you'll learn in this book applies to men of all ages. Even men older than 45 will still behave the same way as younger men. They have a little bit more life experience, but as I always say, an old monkey is still a monkey.

I have a couple of basic rules if you want to get the most out of this book. The first rule is that you should *never ever* believe a word I write. Everything I say will be wrong. If you have that mindset, it will be a lot easier to remember everything that you're reading. If every time you say to yourself, "OK, is this correct?" Then you'll find proof in my relationship theory by examining the connections you've had with men or the relationships you've seen your friends have.. I simply challenge you to always search for proof in your own life and the lives of your friends and family as you read my words. That's what is really going to help you. If you look at your life, your past, you will see that quite often you hit an invisible wall especially with men. You're in a relationship. All of a sudden, something changes that makes you feel uncomfortable—you hit a wall. You don't even see that wall, so you think, "Why is he doing that? What's going wrong? What am I doing here?" The goal of this book is to show you the wall.

When you were growing up, you learned a lot of stuff. You learned how to speak, how to get dressed, how to read. You were taught economics. ,Maybe you learned other languages like "Voulez vous coucher avec moi, ce soir?" (yes, I actually speak French in real life); You learned how to solve difficult mathematical equations. But nobody showed you how attraction functions, how you can create it, and how you can keep him attracted. There's no one who said, "Open your books to page 36. Today we are going to talk about attraction." Yet it is one of the most fundamental things in life. This subject became my passion, my specialty, because we're all looking for love one way or another.

"Repetition is the mother of skills" is what Tony Robbins , one of my mentors, always says. That is correct. If you just read this book once, nothing is going to change in your life. You're going to say, "Ah, yes. That's true," but your newfound knowledge will quickly fade and when you are in a relationship with a man, or if you are trying to seduce a man, you will continue to make the mistakes that you've made in the past because it didn't become an automatism yet. If you repeat this book enough, on the other hand, you'll see that when you have an interaction with a man, all of a sudden you will remember concepts and techniques you've learned in this book. You will say, "Ah, that's why this is happening now. If I do this, he will do that. I don't want that result. If I do this, then I get that result, and that's what I want." That's why you have to repeat everything, especially this book.

You are reading this right now because you want to change something in your life. There is something that you are not truly happy with. What you've been doing with men up until today gave you a result that didn't really please you 100 percent. Otherwise, you wouldn't be reading this book. If you keep doing what you've always been doing, you will also always get the same result. If you change something that you are doing, you might get a different result. Some of the things I'm going to explain are going to be weird. You might say, "What? This doesn't make any sense." Obviously, men don't make sense, so you will have that a lot. But please bear with me. Test everything. Play with it. Try to prove me wrong. Not by saying or thinking, "No, this can't be right. I'm going to forget about this," but by doing it—by seeing, testing, playing with it to see if it actually works or not. Open up your mind. Play with it and see what it does.

Are you motivated? Are you ready to get started and finally get men in every sense of the word? Let's go!

Men Are Weird

I'm pretty sure that you know the phrase, "Playing hard to get." Someone invented that phrase because playing hard to get actually delivers; it gives you results. It also feels a little bit strange since you're not really "yourself" when you're playing hard to get. For me, love is not about playing games, but it *is* about playing.

Love is a game. Love is supposed to be exciting. Love is supposed to give you butterflies and knots in the pit of your stomach because you are unsure. Love always comes with uncertainty. If you think back, and you think about all the men whom you've dated and met in your life—I'm willing to put my money on the fact that the men who you had the strongest attraction toward, from your side, were the men whom you were unsure about their feelings toward you. I am not saying that you never loved a man who was very clear that he loved you as well, but those who weren't entirely clear about their feelings, who were more of a challenge—more of a mystery—were more attractive to you. Am I correct?

Remember, I'm always wrong, so please validate what I say. Check if you find examples of this statement in your own life.

So you are attracted the most to the men whose feelings you aren't sure of. Well, the same applies for males. If you want a man to be more attracted to you, we need to add a little bit of uncertainty so the man can't always tell how *you* feel. This isn't really "playing hard to get." We just add some mystery, some uncertainty, something he needs to work for.

Please take a second right now to think about a friend of yours who is really good with men. I don't know if you know someone like that, but if you know a woman who is really good with men, you'll see that she knows how to flirt. Flirting is a game. Good seducers know how to challenge a man. Challenge creates uncertainty and is a game. That friend probably knows how to tease a man. Teasing creates uncertainty and is a game. See? They really know how to use all those ingredients to create some attraction; they know how to play the game.

Those women who are good with men often are naturals. Some women simply know what to do with a man. They started testing at an early age. They had success with trial and error, and they found their way. Some of them have actually studied how to attract and seduce a man, started playing with it, and became naturals. We can learn a lot from those naturals. I've been studying them for a couple of years already. They are really good with men, and you'll see they use a certain system that I'll explain later in this book.

This chapter is called "Men are weird" because they are. Men are very different from women. That's the reason you love a man and not a woman if you are a heterosexual. Most women try to apply their female logic when they're trying to understand a man. Of course, this doesn't work. Using a woman's rationale to explain a man's thinking will always make a man seem illogical; it makes him seem weird.

There are a few reasons why men seem odd to women. First of all, a man is a strange creature because it is quite difficult to see what is going on in his head. The outside often doesn't say anything about the inside. He might seem very distant; it might look as if he doesn't care about something because he's silent, for instance. On the inside, maybe he's very nervous. A woman, however, loves her emotions, and she is quite easily going to show all of them. A man is going to try to hide them.

There's another big difference between men and women. When you as a woman feel that something is wrong with the relationship that you are in, then you are probably going to try to make it work at first. Even if it takes some time, you are going to stick with it because you don't want to quit too fast—you want to give it a chance. A man is different. When a man has a certain click in his head and he sees that this relationship isn't really working out, he's not going to try to make it work. He's going to run away fast. That may seem weird. When a woman ends a relationship, she is usually pretty sure that it won't work out, simply because she's sure she tried it. When she's gone, she's gone for good. Whereas a man sometimes runs away, and only then, he realizes, "Oh, did I do the right thing here? I kind of miss her." And then he comes back. As a woman, you think, "Is he playing with me? What's he doing?" Have you ever had this happen to you, or do you know someone who was in this situation? Quite often, you'll see that the man who actually ran away starts to come back the minute that you don't love him any more. The minute that you find another guy in your life and are ready to forget him. Then, all of a sudden, he sees the light and he knows that he wants you back. Strange, right?

We all want what we cannot have, and we all want what we cannot have anymore. That is a psychological fact. The Counting Crows once had a song that was something like: "Don't it always seem to go that you don't know what you got till it's gone?" Life is exactly like that, if you ask me.

Another reason men are weird to women is because men are very afraid of their emotions. They are scared of feelings. As a child, a man is taught to be strong. He shouldn't show his emotions especially when he has an uptight father, for instance. It is unmanly to do so. That creates two types of men: too nice or too mysterious. The first one is typically a man who missed out on expressing all his emotions when he was young, and became way too emotional when he grew up. That is the type of man who cries, who seeks your approval all the time, and who constantly asks you if you like him because he needs the reassurance. That is the type of man who gives you 700 compliments the first minute of the date. You know this type of guy because this is probably the guy *you* have already dumped. You might have thought that you should like that guy because he's so sweet and nice, but soon there is no attraction, is there? I'm pretty sure that the men you've broken up with came out of this category. They gave you some sort of pressure in the relationship, and they take away uncertainty. Might I be right?

Try to think about a man who did this to you. He was way too sweet, too emotional, too nice. Because of that, you either couldn't fall in love with him, or you fell out of love with him. Men, of course, would have the same reaction. If you do all these things to a man, he's going to feel the same loss of attraction. He's going to run away, even if you seemed to be everything he was looking for at first.

Now the second type of man, the one who is too mysterious, doesn't like emotions whatsoever. He runs away from them. When he feels emotions, he tries to ignore them, and he definitely doesn't talk about them. Sometimes he has a bad mood, simply because he feels emotions and he doesn't like it. This is the type of guy who makes you wonder where you stand and where the relationship is going. Is this the type of guy you might be attracted to? You might think, "I deserve better," or "I need a guy who is clear to me, who shows me his emotions." This is the type of guy who is attractive, isn't it? You might find that strange—so did I in the past, but there's a reason behind all of this.

In this type of male, you will find players, bad boys, and men who treat you badly, but they are not all bad. The right type of man who will actually treat you with respect is also in this exact category. Men out of the first category, the so-called nice guys, simply take away all of the challenge. They would give you a boring relationship where *you* will lose the excitement, the spark, the attraction. Men from the second category give you a relationship with sparkles, with electricity, and with passion. If you'll learn how this type of guy thinks, then you can create an amazing relationship.

Nevertheless, great things don't come easy. The second type of man cannot talk about his emotions, and he doesn't even know how to handle them. If you then ask him any of the following questions: Where is this relationship going? Are you thinking about marriage? Should we live together? Should we get a baby? He doesn't know. He doesn't know what he thinks about those things because they involve emotions. I'm pretty sure this will frustrate you a lot, because you'll think he's insensitive. You might think he does have emotions, but he doesn't want to talk about them. Some types of men are so afraid of these feelings that they don't allow these emotions. They are so afraid of the responsibilities of being in a real relationship, living together, or having a baby that they can't even toy around with the idea in their heads. It overloads their weak emotional system. They don't want to talk or think about it beforehand, they'll deal with it when it happens. That type of man will know he's ready, when he is ready. He won't be able to talk about it beforehand.

This type of man is a foreign concept to women. When you have conversations with your female friends, for example, what do you talk about? Is it possible that you talk about relations, gossip, how people feel, how you feel, etc.?

You probably talk about emotions. Women love emotions. Women love certain movies like *The Notebook*. For a man, that's a very, very difficult movie to watch because it creates way too many emotions.

What type of television series do you watch? Maybe you watch dramas involving many relationships and gossip. Do you know why you like these things as a woman? As a woman, you are designed and destined to deal with emotions. You instinctively know how to do these things. And there's more! You actually love it. You need to feel these emotions and discuss them with other people. But if you look at a man and put him in front of the love drama, *The Notebook*, he's going to feel uncomfortable. He feels all these emotions, and he doesn't know what to do with them.

This is evident when we think about what men talk about when they are together. Women think men talk about women, sex, and sports all the time. They might talk about women; they might talk about money. They will talk about their careers. Maybe about their cars. They talk about "things." When they talk about women, they talk about them as objects. I'm sorry to be brutally honest here. If I ask one of my male friends, "How's your relationship with your girlfriend?" They are always going to tell me "great" or "not so great." They aren't going to give me any details about the emotional part of the relationship. No, we never talk about that. If I ask a male friend, "How was your day at work?" he is going to respond "good" or "That guy just got fired." He's never going to say, "Ya know, I just had to hand that memo to Mike, and he looked at me in a funny way. I don't know why he did that, but it really upset me . . ." He doesn't do that because that's not what a man does. That's what women do.

There is another thing that plays a major role here. When men are together with their friends, they have learned that men shouldn't talk about emotions. They shouldn't feel them or even have them, because when they do and when they show their emotions, their soft side, they will have to endure jokes about it. The other men in the group are going to laugh and say things like "you're such a woman." Sounds crazy, but this is what happens and *that's* why men seem to objectify everything they talk about. It's the masculine way.

Avoiding their feelings is also why he treats you differently than he does when you're both in a group of friends. Have you ever noticed that a man acts different when he is with his friends compared to when he is alone with you? Some women often tell me, "My man is quite macho when he is amongst his friends even when I'm there as his girlfriend or wife, but when he's all alone with me, he's really sweet." Some men have two faces. So please don't take it personally when he's a little bit weird toward you when his friends are near. He is trying to shield off his emotions from them. He wants to be seen as a man and is thinking about his reputation.

In essence, you need to remember that men are afraid of emotions. The type of man who isn't afraid of emotions has a lot of feminine energy and that man is probably the type of man you are not going to feel a lot of attraction toward, at least not for long. Most men, however, are scared of emotions. This may seem weird to you. You love to talk about the future; you love to think about marriage, babies, and houses. The man simply wants to do fun stuff with you. He wants to go on great dates with you; he wants to feel good with you. **He wants to feel better while being with you than without you.** Otherwise, he wouldn't stay. But he doesn't want to talk about all those emotions, and he doesn't want to talk about how good he feels when he's with you. He doesn't care where the relationship is going. He will see it when the relationship gets there. That's harsh, right? But I find it important to tell it like it is. Please reread this paragraph because it's vital that you understand this major difference between men and women.

Are you starting to feel the very big difference here? This is what a man is looking for. He wants to have fun; he wants to have fun with you. He wants to feel great with you *without* talking about it. The talking part is what scares him, not the emotional connection with you in itself. He likes to have an emotional connection with you; he just doesn't want to talk or even think about it. You, however, probably do want to talk about it. You do want to hear from him that he loves you and that everything will be all right. You need to hear it in words, he needs to say it. Showing isn't enough. You probably need to hear it. Am I correct? Most women are looking for that certainty. They need it in 'writing.' That's a big incompatibility, because if you really want to talk about it, you scare him away. When you talk about your feelings, some men are going to say that you are oversensitive and are going to run away. This is a childish mistake as well, in my opinion. Even if it is difficult for a man, he should do his best for you, he should be able to see your point of view as well, just as you should see his. The effort must come from both sides, of course.

There is a way in between; there is a way where you mix things up a little bit and find a solution where both parties are happy. I will discuss that solution after the next chapter where I list the biggest mistakes that women make.

So yes, you can scare a man away if you try to push him to show his emotions. When you ask a man, "Why don't you text me back when I text you?" or "Why didn't you call me back? I left you a message" that is an emotional question for a man. I'm sure it isn't for you, but it is an emotional question to him. Some men will respond; some men will lie when they give you an answer. Some men will be so afraid that they just take a very big distance from you and you will never hear from him again, however stupid that may sound.

You cannot change him. You cannot transform him into the type of guy who loves to talk about his emotions. All women who have ever tried to change a man have failed. Think about women you know who have tried to transform the guy they were dating. Sometimes it seems they have succeeded, because the guy seems like he's changed. A couple of months, sometimes a couple of years later, you actually see that he hasn't, and they break up. You can't change him.

What you can do, however, is change yourself. Change the way your react to things. Change the stories you tell yourself when something is happening to you. Every story that you tell yourself during a situation is going to give you a certain emotion. Let me give you an example of a stupid story. The first time I was in California, I was standing in front of a red light in the right lane, ready to turn right. The lights were red. I was standing there, and all of a sudden, the guy behind me starts to honk his horn. So I have to tell myself a story to explain what's happening. I say, "People in California are rude. I'm just standing here; it's red, and they honk. What is wrong with these people?" And I felt bad. That was the story I told myself and it made me feel bad about "the people in California." I tell this story to the hotel concierge, and the guy says, "Well here in California you can turn right, even when the lights are red." Now that's something that we never do in Europe. So I had told myself the wrong story and had had a bad feeling or emotion because of this. After I changed the story in my head, Californians were cool again.

See? The stories you tell yourself concerning everything that a man does will define how you feel in the relationship. It's not up to the man to decide how you feel, it's up to you. YOU decide how you react with your thoughts to everything that happens. And the thoughts or stories you choose will define what you will feel on an emotional level. You have more power and control than you might realize.

Sometimes you will tell yourself stories that will mess up the relationship. Let me give you another example. (Rachel is the name of the woman I'm going to use in all of my stories.)

Rachel is dating a guy, Brad, and they've been together 7 months already. She's 34; he's 38. They both have their own apartment. After a date they had, Rachel is sitting at home alone because Brad went to his own apartment. She says to herself, "C'mon, we've been dating for seven months. He lives in his apartment; I live here, but I'm quite often over there. Why don't we start living together? Isn't he supposed to bring up this subject himself?" She thinks, "Where is this relationship going? Do we have a future? Are we ever going to live together? Are we ever going to get married? I need to know these things! There must be something wrong with him. I need to talk to him about this to actually see how he feels. **I need certainty**." Do you know women like Rachel? Maybe very personally? In this example, it's very clear that Rachel really wants to live together. In her mind, everything is sorted out. They're ready for it. She forgets to look at it from his perspective, however. She simply decided something must be wrong with him, since he still hasn't asked for her to move in with him.

The man will not be ready simply because you are. It can be frustrating when you want something and the other person has a different need or want. That obviously is going to happen a lot in relationships. If the both of you always wanted to have the same things, relationships would be utterly boring. No, that's not what's supposed to happen. This may seem strange, but you actually need that insecurity — even though you probably disagree and don't like that feeling. Sometimes there will be incongruence between what you want and what your man is willing to give you. Rachel, in my example, is looking for certainty and wants him to say, "I think we should go live together. Two years from now we can have kids; and then we are going to buy that house, and live happily ever after." That's what she wants to hear. She wants to know that there is a future for the two of them. The problem is that most men don't think that far ahead and when you force them, they will feel their fear of commitment. This is a dangerous fear, since most men run away from it.

There is a type of man who can think about the future and talk about his emotions, the first type of man we discussed earlier. This is the ideal man, on paper at least. When you are on a first date with that guy, he might bring flowers. He might say that he actually wants to get married and wants 3.4 kids with you, the woman he'd been looking for all of his life. He probably already knows the names of those kids. He wants lots of sex with you, and he wants a great life together. Sure, I'm exaggerating here to prove my point; maybe he's not that obvious and just compliments you while looking into your eyes the way a sweet little puppy looks at you. That is the nice guy. A nice guy is the kind of man who knows what a woman wants to hear, and he is going to say all of those things simply to please her. Of course, because of all that, all the attraction will be gone on your side. Maybe not at first, but the physical and emotional attraction *will* start to decline on your end. That's the guy you just need to break up with though you may not understand why you just don't "love him like that" any longer. He seems like everything you want . . .

Nice guys are great friends, but they are no fun in long-term relationships. They mysteriously kill every bit of attraction and challenge. There's no mystery, no intrigue, when you know exactly how they feel about you. I know these nice guys pretty well, because up until the age of 19, I was that nice guy. I tried to please women and was constantly seeking for their approval. I thought that was the right thing to do.

In general, remember one thing. Don't ask for his explanation; don't ask for his words. As long as he keeps meeting you, as long as he keeps going out on dates, or stays married to you, or comes home with a smile on his face because he is happy to see you— he doesn't have to talk about all of those things. The simple fact that he does all of these means that he loves you. Don't mind his words, look to his actions to see how happy he is with you or how unhappy he is with you. Words don't have the value most people give them. It's easy to lie using words; it's a lot harder to lie using actions. It's easy for a man to say "I love you" even when he doesn't. It's a lot harder for him to actually hug you, kiss you, and spend time with you when he doesn't love you. **Try to look more at his actions and place less value on his words**.

The 7 Biggest mistakes most women make with men

There are some mistakes that you might make that can scare a man away. Later on I will dig into the details, but right now I'm going to drop a little grenade and list the biggest mistakes you can make in a relationship. If you make one of these mistakes, the man is going to feel less and less attracted to you—to the point where he starts to take some distance and starts to run away.

Mistake One: why so serious?

Some women try to make things too serious too soon. Some men are afraid to commit. I'm willing to put my money on the fact that the men you are attracted to are the ones who are often afraid to commit. Do you know how I know this? All the men who have been chasing you, who you don't want to be in a relationship with, are not afraid to commit. They want you, and they want to please you. They're the nice guys; they're very clear about their feelings toward you. That's probably why you don't like them (maybe without even being aware of it). Again, that's the kind of guy who is very sweet and wants to marry you after the first date. He wants to live happily ever after with you. If you are not attracted to that type of guy, by definition you are attracted to the type of man who is a little bit more afraid to commit to you, who's more of a challenge and harder to keep. Please keep in mind that everything I say is wrong; and you always have to question everything I say. Is my previous statement correct. Do you agree? Because this is quite a predicament. The man you're most attracted to is the type of men who will not give you what you are looking for: certainty. If he would, *you* might lose interest!

When a woman makes things too serious too soon, the man is afraid. This doesn't mean that all men are looking for one-night stands. What they are looking for is a chase. *They* want to convince you to take it to the next level; they actually

Keephimattracted.com

want to work for it. If everything is too easy too soon, then it simply doesn't feel right for a man. There's no fun anymore.

Mistake Two: happy hunting!

The second mistake happens when a woman doesn't allow a man to chase her. Might it be possible that men are the ones who invented sports and that women joined the game of sports later on? Tennis for instance, was a sport exclusively for men at first. Tennis for women came later on. Same with boxing, bicycle riding, fishing, golf, etc. Men are ambitious and want to hunt and win, it's in their DNA ever since "man" started to walk instead of crawl centuries ago. They want "more," and they want to fight for it. I'm not a sexist; I realize that you are ambitious as well, and that there are very good female athletes out there. I realize this, but I'm talking about the real ambition to win. That is manly energy. When you see a woman succeed at those things, she's using her male energy (achieving) instead of her female energy (emotions).

I don't know if you participate in some kind of sport, but if you do—why do you do it? Is it possible that you like to participate because it's fun, and you like to be around other people when you practice that sport? That might be the case. Most women who don't compete in sports at the highest level do it because they want to have fun. It's not about winning for them, it's about having fun.

Keephimattracted.com

Why do men participate in sports? They want to win. They want to knock the other person to the ground and walk all over him. Even a "friendly" football match can quickly become a testosterone-rich environment where every man really wants victory. To men, it's not about fun, it's about winning. That's the big difference. A man is programmed to be competitive, to be the best, better than all the other ones. Almost every man has this to a certain extent. You have the nerdy type of guy who wants to win during a game of Call of Duty on his game console or computer. You have guys who play in the NFL and really want to beat the other team by as many points as possible and so on.

Why do men participate in or watch sports? Because they might lose. They like the excitement of the fact that they have to do their best to win, or that their favorite team has to do their best to win. **The possibility of losing has to be there**. It has to be exciting.

Why is it that men want to win, compete, and fight? That actually started when men were competing for a woman. Yes, it's true! When you study animals in the wild, you'll see that the male animal is going to fight with another male animal to win the interest of the female. Deer, birds, some types of fish, they all fight. Even monkeys fight! They all fight to get laid, to get the love, to procreate. Humans do this as well.

Imagine you're in the year 1600. There's a princess sitting on her throne, and there are two men on horses. They both have a very long, sharp pole. They start racing toward each other on their horses. They know there's only one winner. One gets brutally knocked of his horse; the other one gets the princess or at least a kiss. It's probably the one with the longest pole who wins (no pun intended). That instinct still exists in every man. Men do the picking; women do the choosing, as I'll explain in a later chapter. They had to fight to impress a woman, but there is more.

In ancient times, the leader of the village would be a man. That man was responsible for everyone and everything in that village. He had to make sure there was food; he had to make sure the village was well protected from dragons, ghosts, and goblins. To get that food on the plate, for instance, the men had to hunt. Chasing something, hunting after something is also in his instinct. Now why do men like the chase? Some men still chase; they hunt and fish, etc. Why do they do this? Let's say Mike is a hunter. Imagine that he is hunting after a razorback, a kind of pig. Do you think he would find the hunting process interesting if the razorback would come out and say, "Hey you! Mike! I'm right here. Shoot me please! Shoot me! How do you want me to stand? Like this?" No! That would take away all the challenge. Some men love to hunt because it's difficult. They want the reward and are willing to work for it.

Women are not that different. Just imagine you are watching a so-called chick flick like *The Notebook* or another romantic movie. Have you ever noticed how those stories always go? A man and a women meet. They kiss, and they live happily ever after. The end. No, of course not! That would be boring. Or maybe does it go like this: A man and a woman meet; they kiss, but then something happens. The woman asks, "What? Was I just a stupid bet?" Or the man says, "What? Were you just pretending to be in love with me because you actually work for the CIA?" Whatever the reason is, something goes wrong. There's a major challenge. As a woman, you might think, "Oh my gosh, I hope this turns out all right! This is so exciting! Will they end up together?" Right? Both sexes like excitement. We don't know how it's going to end. We need the uncertainty. Men need it when they watch sports; you need it when you watch *The Notebook.* That's the reason why it is so difficult to stay in love or to fall in love when a man is way too sweet and gives you way too much attention. There's no uncertainty. On the other hand, the guys who make you think: "Does he love me back?" are the ones you fall for. Might I be correct?

We all want what we cannot have, because once we really have it completely, there is no tension anymore. There's no more excitement. The magic is gone. Might it be possible that love, tension, and excitement belong together? Love without tension, excitement, or uncertainty isn't love anymore. I think that's the big secret. Men watch sports or participate in sports, because they don't know who is going to win. It's uncertain, and that makes it so exciting. Try this: if you ever see a man watching a game on television that is not live and you already know who wins, tell him the outcome. See if he continues to watch the game with the same passion. Of course not! The uncertainty, the key ingredient, will be gone.

Please remember that a man wants to show his best self to you, so you will pick him over another man. He wants to fight for you. If you don't allow him to chase, if you're like that razorback saying, "I'm right here! If you want to sleep with me, just ask for my number and I'll go home with you. If you want to marry me, I've been waiting for you all my life" then you'll sadly take away that challenge—even if you're not that obvious and only give him some hints. However, when you keep a little of uncertainty on the table, he will have to keep trying to gain and keep your approval. He'll have to continue to hunt a little bit. This is the secret to natural attraction, even in long-term relationships.

We always want we cannot have, what we cannot have entirely, or what might be taken away or leave us any second.

Here's an example. Let me presuppose you would love a certain pair of shoes. I bring you a pair of those shoes, in your size, and say: "Okay you can have these for the rest of your life." You're going to find them very nice for about a week before you're dreaming of something else. But when I

Keephimattracted.com

say, "You can have this pair of shoes, but someday they are going to disappear and you will never ever get them back," then you will continue to find it exciting to wear them, always, even many months later because every single day might be the last time you get to wear them. Am I correct? Do not make mistake number two. Allow him to chase you.

Mistake Three: Certainty kills attraction

My shoe example brings me to the third mistake, which is taking away all the uncertainty and mystery.

Let's continue with the shoe example and go over it again quickly. Let's say you really love a certain type of shoe. I give you a pair, and I say, "You can have them for the rest of your life." After a couple of months of wearing them, the excitement will be gone. It won't be special to wear those shoes anymore. But if I say, "At some point, I don't know when, they will vanish," is it possible that it remains exciting to wear them? Every time you wear them might be the last time. Imagine that a man is in a relationship with you, and he knows that you like him, but a little voice in his head continuously says, "Every date or every morning that I wake up next to her might be the last moment that I have with her." Do you think this guy will ever cheat on you? Do you think he will ever run away if he has that feeling? His attraction should stay high if the relationship stays exciting, if there is uncertainty. You'll need to implement this idea in your relationship if you want your man to stick around.

Think about the type of guy you like. What is your type of man? Is it possible that it is the type of man who makes you daydream and wonder about him. You wonder what he's doing for a living; you wonder what he's like, what he thinks, etc. There are so many unanswered questions; there's a lot of mystery. There are things that you don't know about him. Is it possible that you are more attracted to the type of guy who makes you think, "Is he going to fall for me?" compared to a man who already told you he likes you several times? That mystery, that uncertainty, is very important from the very first second you meet until the very last second of your relationship. This feeling is important for you, but it's very important for a man as well.

Why does a certain man want to seduce you? He's unsure about your feelings. He wants you, but he is also a little bit unsure and doesn't know if you will actually fall for him. He asks you out for a date, and he thinks, "Yes! I didn't think she was going to say yes, but I have her! Okay we are going to go on that first date. Where should I take her?" A the end of the first date, he thinks, "I really want to kiss her, but is she going to turn her face away? Yes or no?" Five months later he wonders, "I actually want her to move in with me. I'm going to ask her tonight. I hope she says yes, but I don't know . . ." You see? That's what a man wants. If he sits with you in the car and he thinks, "Of course she's going to kiss me back.

She's been all over me all night! She's given me many hints that she likes me, and I know she is looking for a guy like me. I'm even sure she would want me to join her for a night cap." . . . the passion is gone. There is no uncertainty, no challenge. Some men might still kiss you because they simply want you for one night. My guess is that you're not looking for that. You want a true, real relationship with a man who has an emotional bond with you. For that, you need to create that uncertainty in his mind. It has to be more than sex. So how do you get into a relationship and at the same time keep things a mystery, keep the man uncertain? How difficult is that? Let me give you a couple of examples.

Adam is the guy who I'm going to use in my examples right now. Adam is the perfect type of man. He's Prince Charming. He's the guy on the white horse. He's everything you've been looking for since the first day of high school when you dreamed about your future.

Adam, the perfect man, has a second date with Rachel. Adam has seen prettier women than Rachel. She's attractive, but he has seen prettier. There's something to her; there's something about her and he can't put his finger on it. She smiles a lot, and she gives him a great feeling inside. Adam likes that feeling; he likes to feel good. He likes to have fun. She said yes when he asked her out, so he knows that she likes him at least a little bit. Otherwise, she wouldn't be there. But how much does she like him? If he tried kiss her, would she kiss him back? It's exciting because of all that uncertainty, all that mystery. Rachel has not revealed all of her feelings to Adam, therefore, the attraction is high between them. The uncertainty is the key.

Here is a different story. Adam, still the perfect man, has a second date with Rachel. Adam has seen prettier woman than Rachel, but there's something wrong with her. She talks a lot about herself, and it looks like she is trying to impress him all the time. She's also said that Adam is a gorgeous man three times already, and that she's really happy that he asked her out because she didn't expect him to. Now it's especially that last phrase, "she didn't expect him to," that is weird to Adam. He wonders, "Does this mean I can do better than Rachel? If I know how to seduce her that fast then I'm sure I can get prettier women as well." There's no excitement anymore to Adam, and he thinks: "I'm looking at a game on television, and I already know who won. I won! You know what? It's been a long time since I've had sex, so I'm going to have sex with her tonight; and tomorrow I'm simply not going to call her anymore." What an asshole, right? I promise that Adam is the same guy in my two stories. The only real variable in my story is Rachel. She changed. In the first example, she created a lot of attraction and an emotional bond. In the second example, she made it too easy for him. This shows how easily it can go wrong in the beginning of the relationship.

What happens when you are already three years into a relationship? Adam and Rachel have been in a relationship for three years. Rachel works at a large bank. Tonight she has a reception at work, and she couldn't take Adam with her. Husbands and boyfriends were not invited. Adam is watching the Super bowl. He's at home; he has his friends with him. For some reason, he's not enjoying the Super bowl. He's thinking about Rachel: "Maybe she's talking to other men. Did you see that dress she was wearing this morning? It was so sexy. Obviously, there are going to be other men at this party . . . When I texted her this afternoon, it took her five hours to text me back. Five hours! That's too long. There's probably nothing going on, but it's exciting with all this uncertainty." Do you think that Adam is madly in love with Rachel in my example? Let's look at a different variation.

Adam and Rachel are still three years into a relationship. Rachel works for a very large bank. Tonight she has a reception at work and significant others were not invited. Adam is watching the Super bowl with his friends. He's having fun. He wonders, "The new receptionist we have at work, was she really smiling at me or was she smiling at someone else today? I kind of like her." He doesn't think about Rachel at all. She already texted him five times today to tell him that she's thinking about him and that she'll miss him tonight. Why would he worry? Do you think Adam is madly in love in this example? I promise, it's still the same Adam in both examples. It's Rachel who is different.

Some men are bad guys and should be avoided; they have no respect for women. Adam does respect women, but like every man he responds to challenge, mystery, and uncertainty. Do you see and feel the difference? The difference lies hidden in the small things in these examples. In the first example, there's always a little bit of uncertainty, a little bit of excitement. Adam knows that Rachel loves him, but she doesn't overdo it. In the second example, she actually overdoes it. There is no uncertainty, no excitement whatsoever. He has to search for that excitement elsewhere ,. . . with the receptionist, for instance. It seems like Adam is a bad guy here. He isn't. Let's be honest, women behave the same way. When a woman has a secure relationship with a man who tells her he loves her every day, it's great, but there is no excitement anymore. So some women are going to look for excitement elsewhere. Some. I'm not saying that you are like that, but both genders have this need for some excitement. If you become an open book, if you show your emotions and your feelings too much and too soon, there's no excitement left, and the natural attraction will die.

Mistake Four: "I'm just going to say it anyway"

Mistake number four occurs when the woman has no self-control. Self-control is very important in life. Studies have shown that people who have self-control have much more successful lives. When you don't have self-control, you will show all your emotions and/or you will act upon them without thinking. When you have angry feelings, you're mad and you show it. When you feel happy, you're happy and you

Keephimattracted.com

show it. You continuously show all of your emotions. There is no filter on it.

I once had a first date with a woman I liked at first. She was my type, and we had had an interesting conversation. After the first date, it was very clear that she wanted to kiss me. She then called me on my cell phone the morning after our first date. I was working so I couldn't pick up. Four minutes later she calls me again. Five minutes later a different number calls me. Five minutes after that, I get a text message explaining that the other number was hers as well because she was using a different phone. I didn't pick up, because her behavior freaked me out. She didn't have self-control. She wanted to talk to me and when she couldn't because I didn't pick up right away, she began to speed things up and call me more and more. Men are afraid of that. They walk away. This was an obvious example, but some women show they have no self-control in other, less obvious ways.

Think of the opposite: a stable woman who is emotionally mature, knows how to hide her emotions and change her emotions sometimes. That's a different story and that is very attractive to a man. Let me give you some examples:

Rachel is in a relationship with Adam. She wonders, "Does he really love me? You know what, I'm going to send him a little text message simply to see if he responds to it. I'm not going to ask him if he loves me, but I'm going to text him to see if he responds. By doing that, I can see if he loves me."

She clearly needs a little bit of attention. After one hour, Adam still hasn't texted her back, so she texts him again. She asks him, "Did you receive my first message?" Because of this, Adam starts to change how he feels toward Rachel. He doesn't know why, it just happens on a subconscious level.

Rachel and Adam are sitting at table. It's their first date! She wants to tell him that she likes him, because that's how she feels. She thinks, "I'm not going to play any games. I'm going to be myself, so I'm going to show him that I like being here with him." And that's exactly what she does. She says, "I like being with you, Adam." Adam is happy, and he smiles which makes Rachel think, "That went great! It makes him happy when I do that, so I'm going to give him some more of that." So every now and then, she gives him a little hint. She gives him a little compliment simply to get his smile in return. Adam starts to feel a drop in his emotions and feelings toward Rachel. He doesn't know why, but it just happens.

I'm sure something similar has already happened to you or someone you know. It's frustrating that things happen this way, but it's the reality we need to understand and adapt to . Wouldn't it be more fun if we could simply be ourselves 100 percent of the time? Yes and no. In my examples, Rachel has a lack of self-control. It was very clear in the first example with the text messages. If you try to keep the conversation alive by adding questions when you are texting to a man, he knows why you're doing that. Not if you do it once, but if you continue to add a question in every message, just to make sure you get a reply back, he sees your strategy. This kills the uncertainty, the challenge. Now in my last example, they were on their first date. There were multiple mistakes in that example. The mystery and the uncertainty were totally gone, because Rachel gave too many hints. She made it too obvious too soon that she likes him. That was the deadly mistake. "I like you" can mean a lot of things, so that was okay. It actually made Adam happy. If that had been it, Adam would wonder, "She likes me, but how much does she like me?" But no, she continues to give hints and takes away the challenge. She continues to seek his approval and to get a reaction from him. And he feels that, of course. He feels that he is in control of *her* emotions, that she wants something from him. That is something a man doesn't want to feel. Since she continues to give compliments and hints, the tension is gone. The love is gone.

Think about the men who have lost interest in you or a friend of yours, and try to analyze the first dates you had. Was there self-control, or not? Self-control simply means that you learn how to manage your emotions and think before you act upon them. In a famous marshmallow test, young kids are given one marshmallow. The kid sits at a table, and there is one adult woman in the room as well. She gives the kid one marshmallow and says: "If you can wait and not eat it until I return, you get a second one." She then leaves the room. A camera records everything that happens in the room, and every kid reacts in a different way. Some simply eat the marshmallow right away. They have no self-control at all and want instant gratification. Other kids try to exert some self-control. They hide the marshmallow, close their eyes, hold their hand in front of their eyes so they can't see the marshmallow and cannot be tempted. They know that using self-control will give them more later, since a second marshmallow will follow if they don't eat the first one until the lady comes back. Most of these kids who took part in the original test have been followed throughout their lives and were more successful in every area of life, be it financially, professionally, or romantically.

If you don't have self-control then it might be worth working on it. Think about the future impact of your actions when it comes to a man and relationships. Think: "If I do this now, will it hurt the relationship in the long term or not?" Here's a simple example. You've just had a first date with a man, and it went well. He kissed you at the end of the date and you feel great. You've been longing for him for a while now, and you want to share those emotions. You're also a little unsure. Did he like it as well? This uncertainty makes you feel uneasy, so you want to fix it and you text him, "I loved our date yesterday and I think I really like you. I'm still thinking about our kiss. Did you like it too and can I see you again tonight?" This is an example of not using self-control and searching for instant gratification. Most men will not respond well to a message like this, especially so fast after only the first date. Many mistakes I previously discussed are hidden in this one text message as well. It takes away the mystery; it doesn't allow him to chase you or to wonder you liked it and when should he ask you out again. Will you still want to see him? It simply doesn't allow *his* attraction to grow.

A woman with self-control would think: "Gosh, I feel uncertain. Where is this going? I loved our kiss, and I want to be with him ever since I met him at work 2 months ago, and I'm so close now. Does he feel the same? Should I text him and see how he responds? No, I'll wait. If he liked me he will contact me and ask me out again." This, for instance, would keep the mystery intact, the intrigue, the challenge, and all of the other elements that are so important during the first stages of any romantic relationship.

Mistake Five: If I tell him I like him, he'll like me more

Mistake number five is closely related to the other ones. It's when a woman wants to make a man feel how much she likes him or how much she loves him. When you fall for someone, strange things happen. You get a lot of emotions. You get butterflies in the stomach; you might lose your appetite and feel stressed. But what have we learned? Men have a difficult time with emotions. So when a man falls in love, for him it is ten times more difficult. He has a very hard time controlling himself and all of those emotions of love. When you're madly in love, it's easy to lose self-control (mistake number 4). Some men have this when they fall madly in love with you. You'll see that they don't know what to do with themselves. They start giving you compliments; they tell you how much they like you and become way too nice and accommodating. You are probably going to fall out of love after a couple of weeks when a man reacts like this because then *he* is taking away all the mystery.

As a woman, the same thing happens. All of a sudden, you want to make him see how much you like him. I might be wrong, but my guess is you especially want to tell him all of those things if you think he doesn't like you as much as you like him. Some women, who are unsure of whether or not their love interest likes them, will start to show their emotions, give hints, and give compliments simply to reveal their feelings. Those women think, "I like you and when I tell you, you'll like me, too." It doesn't work like that. A man is afraid of that. There's no insecurity or challenge left.

Imagine that you like a man and you know that he likes you, too. You kind of know that he already loves you a little bit. He wants to be with you, asks you out on dates and the two of you have fun together. If, at that point, you show no emotions whatsoever, he is going to fight for you like you've never seen a man fight for you. Playing hard to get like that would not be nice, because that would be taking advantage of "the system of love." Nevertheless, that's how it works. If you don't show him any emotions whatsoever and he likes you, he's going to start to chase after you, to seek validation, and to get some emotions from you. He wants you to respond. He is going to want to fight for your approval. He is going to become weak, become a nice guy simply to prove to himself that he can get you. That's strange, right? Even macho men start to behave like this when a woman stops caring and doesn't show her emotions any longer. I'm sure you've seen this happen in real life. A woman loves a man but he's not committed. She leaves him and minutes, hours, or days later the man transforms into a caring man, confessing his love for her. If, however, she takes him back, he morphs into his old self soon after.

We all want what we cannot have, and what we can have forever quickly loses its value. Think about the shoe example I gave earlier on. You will have to find the right mix between "hard to get" and "easy to get." It's very difficult to see where the right mix is, because it's different in every single situation. In general, it's better to show too little emotion than too much to a man. Showing too little will not harm you, showing too much will negatively affect his level of interest in you.

Mistake Six : he's the most important person in my life

Making the man too important in your life is a very big mistake, and I'm sure you've made that mistake before. We all have. I've made that mistake a lot of times, and every time that I did, I had to suffer the consequences. There are multiple reasons why this is a mistake. The first reason is that you take away all the uncertainty. If you make him too important, he doesn't have to wonder whether you like him or not. He knows it. The selection is over. He knows that you've "hired" him and he starts to wonder, "If it is this easy maybe I can get an even better job." You see? That is something that is in our nature. We all want the best we can get and when we really "have" something, we wonder if there's something even better out there.

Let's say I walk into a modeling agency, and I want to seduce a model. So I start to flirt with one and it works immediately. She falls head over heals in love with me. What a miracle, because I'm not that special! Somewhere in my head I'm going to start wondering, "Hmm. If it was this easy, maybe I can get an even prettier super model, for instance." See? Most men really like a Porsche. Once they have one, they start to think about a Ferrari. Once they have a Ferrari, they are going to think about that beautiful Lamborghini. They always want something better than what they already own. That is in our nature. You might have the same reaction.

Keephimattracted.com

A relationship can stay enticing and exciting when both parties never 'own' each other. When you are in a long-term relationship with a man and he knows that you like him but he isn't the most important thing in your life, his instincts are going to keep reminding him that he has to do his best to keep you. When he can't take you for granted, when you are someone who might walk away someday, he is going to say, "Okay, I need to do my best. I need to work out, be affectionate and respectful to make sure that I keep her."

Sometimes you'll see a woman who complains about her man. She'll say, "He plays computer games the entire day. He doesn't organize his sock drawer. He leaves the toilet seat up." When you analyze those women, you'll see that their man is the most important thing in their lives. They quite often don't have a lot of hobbies; they don't have a lot of friends. They don't have a lot of stuff to do outside of the relationship. Their man knows this. He thinks, "Why should I put in an effort? If I want to play games all day or watch TV every time I'm home, I can! If I want to leave the toilet seat up, I will! She's not going to run away." The behavior of this very same guy would be totally different once he has the feeling that he actually has to fight for her. Many movies handle this topic (*The Break-Up* with Jennifer Aniston for instance). When the woman changes *her* behavior and leaves, she creates the ultimate challenge. All of a sudden, the guy starts to fall for her again, and then you see what an effort he does to get her back.

Keephimattracted.com

Now the second reason why it's very difficult and perhaps dangerous to make the man the most important thing in your life is his fear of commitment. This might even be the most important reason. Let me give you a couple of examples out of my personal life. When I was younger, I had a dog. He was my best and most loyal friend. I trained that dog very well. So when I was 29, I decided it was time for a new dog. I went to the store, and I bought a Labrador puppy. I bought everything for him: funny toys, a basket, a nice pillow. I was watching television that very first evening. The little puppy Labrador positions himself right in front me. He looks at me with his sweet, little eyes…. All of a sudden, I had a very strange feeling going through me. That feeling said, "Uh oh, you do realize that for the next 13-15 you are going to be the most important thing in this dog's life. If you don't feed him, he dies. If you don't take him outside, he poops around the living room. You're his everything. You'll be *the* most important thing in his life." I knew I was going to have different girlfriends over the next fifteen years, but the dog was always going to be there. I could no longer leave on vacation just like that. I would have to find someone to take care of the dog and would feel guilty or miss him. I got all these emotions in my head, all that responsibility started to weigh on me and as a man, it was very difficult to deal with them. I realized that I was too important for that dog. The pressure on my shoulders, the responsibility, became so big that I brought him back to the store the next day. I swear, and that is not easy to admit here, that I had been crying the whole way to the store. The puppy sat next to me and looked at me the whole time practically saying, "Why don't you want to keep me? I don't understand." I had red, puffy eyes when I gave the dog back. I told the store owner that my girlfriend was allergic to dogs and I didn't know that. It was an excuse. I was too afraid to commit, and yet I loved the dog. He made me too important in his life. It wasn't his fault; I just wasn't ready yet.

I can't help but wonder what would have happened when someone would have asked me to look after the dog for 2-3 weeks with no strings attached. I'm sure I would have kept it. But that one moment freaked me out so much that I ran—another proof that men are stupid when it comes to commitment. The story is real, I'm not a bad guy, and yet most men can get that "I've got to get out of here" feeling at any second. I didn't even see it coming.

This is very important to understand. Sometimes you are going to find a man who really loves you, but the minute you make him feel like he is the most important thing in your life, he will feel the very same pressure and might run away from it *even if he loves you*. Remember that my little dog story might have been entirely different if someone had told me, "You can keep the dog for three months. If you don't like him, you can give him back. We can erase his memory so he doesn't miss you." I wouldn't have brought him back. The reason I brought him back within 24 hours was because I cared. I didn't want him to attach himself to me, because then I wouldn't be able to give him away anymore. I felt trapped

Keephimattracted.com

and was afraid to commit. Guess what I would've done at the end of the three months? Of course, I would have kept the dog. I would have fallen in love with him. I wouldn't have given him away for all the money in the world because he would have bypassed my commitment radar! Because there were no strings attached, I wouldn't have been afraid to commit because there was no pressure. I would have been committed to the dog without consciously deciding to do so. It would have just happened.

If you start a relationship with a man, give him the feeling that "all is okay" and that there's no pressure whatsoever. You want him to think that you're not looking for anything serious *yet*. You then give him the time to fall for you. He will not be afraid to commit, because there won't be any commitment. If I had that dog during the three-month trial period, the dog would still be with me every day. There would be a commitment, but in my head, in my primitive male brain, I wouldn't even see it as a commitment because I have the freedom to bring him back whenever I want.

You can live with a man, and he doesn't get any fear of commitment. He's there every day and doesn't think about leaving. When you start to talk about the relationship and "where it is going," too soon, then you might scare him. Then all of a sudden his commitment-radar starts to beep loudly since he sees the walls closing in on him. It's stupid, but it happens all the time.

Let me give you another real-life example. One of my best girlfriends fell in love with a married man who works where she works. He is fifteen years older than she is, and he is part of the management team. Two years ago, he made it very clear to her that he actually likes her. She liked him too, but he was married and he already had kids. Because of that, they simply flirted a little bit, sent some text messages to each other, and that was it. She knows that I give relationship advice and came to me for help. I could see that the more important she made him, the more distant he became. That was quite logical in that situation. He felt the emotional pressure and knew, "Oh my god, she's really falling for me. I have a wife and a kid, and this is not healthy. I need to take a step back." That's the game of push-and-pull. If you push, the other one is going to run away. If you pull and take a step back, the other one is going to come after you.

After a couple of months, that friend of mine really wanted to spend the night with him, just one night. That was too much for him. He was afraid of that. So she bluffed and told him: "I want to stop doing all of this. I want to stop the flirting. This has no future, and I'm going to invest my time in another man with whom I can have a future." A couple of hours after explaining this to him, the doorbell rang at her house. Guess who was there? It was a very spectacular night, so I was told. Right now, he's divorced and they live together with one daughter and a son on the way. He was the guy who was afraid to commit, she used my advice and played it really well with lots of self-control. As a result, she bypassed his radar and got the big award in the end.

What had happened? Why the sudden change? He felt as if he was too important to her at first. He thought: "I can do whatever I want here, and she's still going to chase me. Whatever I do, however long I need to decide between her and my wife, she's going to wait for me because she loves me." Again, he's not a bad guy. It's simply because my friend allowed this behavior that he did it. He had the power and all of a sudden, she took the power away by saying: "I'll end this. This has to stop right now. You are not important anymore. I'm going to leave and find another man. You don't exist anymore." She didn't use those words, but this is what he was hearing at that time. Something clicked in his head. The fear of commitment became the fear of losing her. Like a crazy man, he started to chase her and he even forgot about the consequences. That's why he even took the risk of showing up at her door. What if someone else from the company would have been at her house for some reason? He didn't care, he took all of those risks because that's what men who are in love do: they hunt! They go for what they want. Afterward, she never made the same mistake again. She never made him too important in her life.

Now before I go into mistake number 7, let's focus. Think about your own life, and search for some proof for what I've been explaining. Think about the men who you have dumped, who were longing for you and you didn't want them, or you didn't want them anymore. Is it possible that those men were the guys who made you too important in their eyes?

Mistake Seven: being yourself

This is a weird mistake and you might feel a lot of resistance when you hear about it. Are you ready? Mistake number 7 is: being yourself too much. Everyone says, "I just want to be myself." When you hear advice in the dating area, everyone says, "Just be yourself, and it will all be okay." How well did that work out for you in the past? It never worked out for me. I'm not saying that you have to act or become someone else. However, imagine a world where you are totally yourself all of the time. That would mean that you do whatever it is you want to do. When I have to stop in front of a red light, my true self says, "I don't want to stop here." Instead of waiting, I just move on. Let's see how much people like that. The same goes for relationships. When you are truly yourself, it means that every second that you feel love, you share it. Every second that you are disappointed, jealous, or mad—you share and show it. Every time that you're a little bit depressed, you go around telling people, "I'm depressed; I don't like my life." How would that be? Not good, of course. Sometimes you have to learn to hide your emotions, to deal with your feelings, and to practice self-control. I've read a great book about that subject. It's called *Emotional Intelligence* by Daniel Goleman, I'm sure you've heard of Daniel Goleman; he's the one who invented the word "EQ," the emotional sibling of IQ. It's a book that helps you deal with your emotions—to hide them sometimes, or to push them away.

When you take a second and think about all the people you know, you will see people who truly are themselves all the time and show every single emotion that they have. They are quite often not as happy as people who know how to control their emotions. Not being yourself all the time means that when you are jealous, for instance, you don't show it. Sometimes when you're mad, you don't show it. Sometimes when you're crazy about someone, you don't show it or you don't show it 100 percent. If you learn how to give the right dosage of "showing your emotions" and being yourself, you will see that life becomes easier. Am I right?

The Golden Way

In this chapter, I'm going to talk about "the golden way." You have already learned that men and women are different. You want something else out of the relationship than him. You, as a woman, like to talk about things. You like emotions. You like to share things and discuss them. A man, on the other hand, loves to win; he loves to have uncommitted fun. He doesn't like to share or talk about emotions. You can see that a relationship between a man and a woman is quite difficult because of these different wants and needs. If both people in the relationship don't help each other out, there's no real relationship. When you're the only one trying to make it work, there's no relationship. The both of you have got to put in an effort.

As you might have learned the hard way, you can't change him. You can only change yourself and how you react. So that's what we'll work on. Imagine that the man who you are in love with is very selfish, but you are in love with him. What is it that you can do? Are there little tricks that you can use to manipulate him in a kind way and still get things done in the relationship? Those tricks exist.

I've been studying why people do what they do ever since I can remember. Since 2004, it has even been my professional career. It's something that I find very valuable. Why do people do what they do? When you study that and learn to understand the answer, you can change how much you love life. One thing that I've discovered in relationships, especially in romantic relationships, is how you can change the relationship by using empathy. When you understand the other person and have an empathetic mind where you can feel and see a situation through the other's eyes, you get a lot of power. I probably don't even need to tell you that.

You're probably reading this book to understand a specific man, to try to get inside of his head. People who stay in their own heads and only want to look at it from *their* perspective hit that glass wall all the time. They hit their head against it and get hurt over and over again. The funny thing is that they don't know where that wall comes from, because they can't even see the wall. They simply feel the pain.

Everything you say to yourself, *everything*, gives you a certain feeling: a neutral feeling, a bad feeling, or a good feeling. There is a lot of stuff happening around you and your mind continuously tries to give meaning to it. Remember my story about the red light in California? I told myself a story that made me angry and put Californians in a bad light. Let's say that you text your man and he doesn't text you back at all. You will need to tell yourself a story to explain why that just happened. You will need to give it a meaning, an explanation. You automatically ask your brain: "Why did that just happen?" and your brain needs to come up with an answer. What is the story you tell yourself when that happens? Some women will automatically think, "He doesn't like me. Something must be wrong. He's with someone else." That will make them feel bad. Some women will say, "Oh he's probably busy at work, no big deal." Those women will have a neutral feeling. It's the same fact that just happened, but they both feel totally different because of the stories they told themselves.

The stories that you tell yourself will define how you will feel and how you will act in the relationship. You hold the key, the power to your own feelings and emotions. It's not the man, it's how you react and what self-talk you'll use that defines everything.

So it is crucial to tell yourself the right kind of story, and I've developed a method to help you do that. I call it: "the friend method." I invented the friend method a while back for another coaching program that I have. The friend method allows you to get an objective view over something that just happened in your life. It makes it easier to get in the head of the other person. Imagine that your best female friend comes to you and says, "I don't know what's wrong but I've just texted Jim, and it's been five hours and he still hasn't texted me back. What could that mean?" What might your response to that be? Is it possible that you might say, "Don't worry, Jim is probably busy." Now if you were dating Jim, and you just texted him and he hasn't texted you back after five hours, what would you say to yourself? Probably something like this: "Something must be wrong," or "He doesn't love me," or "He is probably with another woman," etc. What I'm trying to point out is that you might react differently if it happens in your life versus the life of a good friend of yours. It's probably easy to figure out what to do when it's someone else's problem, isn't it? And when it happens to you, you're blinded, it feels different and you react in another way. Sometimes you make the wrong decisions simply because you're right in the middle of it, because you can't *see* what the right thing to do is.

"The friend method" allows you to get an objective view. Say the man does something that doesn't make any sense. It hurts your feelings, and you're worrying about that. As long as you stay in your own head, you're going to tell yourself the wrong stories. You're going to talk to yourself the wrong way, and you will probably make yourself feel bad. Because of that, you are probably going to act uptight toward the man, you might even lose self-control. As a result, he is going to lose interest. And maybe then, the little voice in your head will say, "See? I told you so." That's a self-fulfilling prophecy. You get exactly that what you were trying to avoid. If, however, you use the friend method and say, "Okay, I need to take some distance here. I'll just imagine that my best friend came over, and she told me that her man did exactly what my man just did. What would I say to her? It's not about me; it's about her. What would I say to her?" Then you write that down. It's best that you write these things down. It's easier to distance yourself from the situation. You can also analyze what you wrote, and you can learn from it. So you write down what happened but you make it about a friend of yours. Then you write down what type of advice you would give her if she would be in that situation. To end the circle of the friend method, you have to accept the advice that you would give your best friend and give it yourself. That is the difficult part since you will feel some resistance at first. There is probably going to be a little voice inside your head that will say, "You know, my case is a little bit different." It isn't; it really isn't. Apply the exact advice that you would give a friend in that exact same situation. Can you see how powerful this friend method can be? It not only works for relationships, but for whatever problem it is that you have in your life. Think: "If my best friend would come to me and explain that same problem, what would I give as advice?" Because you would be objective, it would be easy to know what to do. It would be clear. Accept that advice, and apply it to yourself. That's the first step.

To make it even better, the second step is that you try to get into *his* head, that you try to see it from his perspective. You'll need to figure out why he might have done what he did. Keep using the friend method at this time; pretend it's not about your guy. It's about the partner of a friend. You still stay outside of your own life, and you'll try to get an objective view of the situation. Let's say that you've been in a relationship for six months and you still don't know what's going to happen in the future. That worries you. In that case, think: "My best friend comes to me and says that she knows a man, and she's been in a relationship for a few months. She doesn't know where this is going." First off, write down how you might give as advice to your friend. Step Two: think about why that guy might not be talking about the future of the relationship and why he's avoiding the subject. "He's probably focusing on his career. He really loves her, but he's focusing on his career, or he is enjoying other hobbies. He doesn't like to talk about the future; he doesn't like to talk about his feelings. He's staying with her, , so he probably loves her . . . and so on. Because of step one, you got out of your own life. You received an objective view and it all seems very clear why that guy might be doing something you don't understand, since it's not about you. So you continue getting into *his* head: "Men are afraid of commitment. Does that mean that he doesn't love her? Of course not! He's still with her."

When this is done, you close the circle again and bring it back to your own life. You then force yourself to realize that's why your man is doing all of those things. Because you step out of your own situation, it becomes easier to focus on the good as well, to calm yourself down, and keep your self-control. What he's doing (or not doing) might be a bad thing, but it also could be positive. This exercise allows you to see different possibilities for you situation, whereas before you were probably only focusing on the negative: "He doesn't love me; he's with other women; this is going nowhere" etc. Of course, both the bad and the good reasons you came up with can all be the real reason why he behaves a certain way. But the good news is you won't be biased and only seeing the negative possibilities. When you take the positive reasons into account as well, you won't become uptight or unhappy. You will remain self-confident.

I do realize it's a difficult exercise. I hope that the next time you're going to read this, you will write the steps down and really try to apply it to the situations that you are having with your man. Really see how you can apply them to your own life, because it will work. You have to practice this a little bit. Repetition is what will make you good at this, and it will change your relationships in ways you cannot even begin to imagine at this point.

The naturals, as I've mentioned before, are very good with men and have great long-term relationships. In their relationships, the man and the woman are happy. These naturals know why a man does certain things. They don't always think about the negative side. Here's a situation I encountered a lot when I coached people on a private basis. The man would come home, and he would have some flowers or another gift with him. Normally, this specific man doesn't do that. Some women immediately think, "Ah! What did he just do? He wants to make up for something. He's cheating on me!" See? That's the type of story they tell themselves. They create fear and use a lot of what-if-phrases. Are they going to be happy in the relationship? No! Are they going to be uptight? Yes! Are they going to be fun to hang around? No! Is the man going to be happy when he is in a relationship with her? Of course not. They create a self-fulfilling prophecy. They try to get the man and keep him attracted, but these women become so uptight because of all the stories they tell themselves that they are no fun to hang around. What kind of

Keephimattracted.com

man would want to stay with a woman like that? They get what they were trying to avoid, hence the self-fulfilling prophecy. That is why the exercise in this chapter is so important.

There are different ways to react, to respond to every situation. I'll talk about them in the next chapter.

Men are Addicted

What are men addicted to? It's nothing illegal; it's nothing that they shouldn't be using. It's you. They're addicted to having fun with you, a woman.

Do you know what conditioning is? Do you know Pavlov and his famous dog? Maybe you do. Pavlov was a Russian scientist who really changed the world of psychology. In one of his experiments, he attached some devices to the dog to measure its saliva production. He would say, "If I put food in front of Bob, the dog, we get extra saliva." So Pavlov puts food in front of Bob the dog, and Bob produces extra saliva. While Pavlov puts food in front of Bob, he rings a little bell. He does that many times. Every time Bob sees and smells food, creates saliva, he hears a bell. After sixty times or so, Pavlov comes into the room without food. All of a sudden, he rings a little bell, the same bell he had been using before. Guess what happened? The dog produced extra saliva. There was no food, but the dog had linked up the bell to the food. He had the same physical reaction.

This is conditioning. Pavlov was able to condition a living creature to do something that previously it wouldn't done—produce extra saliva at the ring of a bell. If he would have rung the bell before the test, before the experiment, the dog wouldn't have done anything. Now he did. This "conditioning" is an amazing concept, because both you and I are conditioned every day. The more you are aware of this, the more you can defend yourself against any unwanted forms of conditioning that try to hijack your emotions.

Because of this type of conditioning, we can link up feelings and emotions to something that didn't give us a feeling before. Do you see where I'm going? I'm going to link Pavlov's dogs to the relationship world. If you can get your guy to link you and "having fun," then he is going to stay with you forever. Men are addicted to having fun.

"We often forget what people told us, but we NEVER forget how they made us feel."

You simply have to program him. When any one of us gets an emotional feeling, we are going to start linking all of the elements that are present at that time to that feeling. When you feel sick after eating something, you'll link it to what you ate, a smell or, something else. When you're happy, you'll link it to the place you were on a vacation, the weather, the people you were with at that time, the current radio hits, etc. So the trick here is to have him link "fun" to *you*!

That's it! Everyone simply wants to have fun. Even Cindy Lauper sang it, "Girls just want to have fun!" It's in our nature to walk away, even to run away, from things that make us feel bad and to be attracted to things that make us feel good. If you make sure that you have fun with your boyfriend or husband then he's going to get addicted to you. Just like the bell gave the dogs saliva, you are going to give him a great feeling every time he sees you or even thinks about you!

So how does this happen? Remember, at first the bell did not create extra saliva for the dog. Because of all the food there was, he started to link up the bell to the food. After sixty times of just that, Pavlov could just ring the bell and the dog would salivate. He could ring that bell even a hundred more times without giving the dog food, and the dog would continuously salivate. He was programmed. The bell made him think of food.

Let's say that a guy just meets you. He doesn't have any feelings for you yet. You are the bell before the experiment, so nothing happens with his emotions when he sees you. You go out with him, and you make it fun. You have a fun date. He starts to feel good. All of a sudden he is going to link you to feeling good. Do that a couple of times and after a while simply thinking about you will make him feel good. Here is the great part about it: This all means that sometimes, even when you are not fun to be around because you're feeling down, he is still going to feel good around you—just as the bell continuously makes the dog salivate even when there is no food. Sometimes when there's no fun, he will still like being around you. See? That's why it is so important to make it fun in the beginning and to make sure the things you do together are interesting and exciting. This means that you should leave your problems at home or share them with your girlfriends, not with him, at first. Do not talk about negative of heavy subjects early in the relationship.

This is one of the examples of where it is better to not "be yourself" completely. You'll probably think, "Well of course I want to be myself. If I have problems, I want to be able to share them with him." Yes, but exercise caution. Don't share your sould with him too soon and definitely not all the time. Make sure there is more fun than bad things in the relationship.

"Everything you make him feel consistently will be linked up to you, it will program him."

So make sure you send out positive vibes most of the time. Don't give him feelings of guilt, for instance. Never say things like, "I thought you loved me. If you loved me, you would have called me back." These things obviously condition him, but in a bad way. When a woman continuously gives 'difficult' emotions to a man, he will be conditioned to think negative thoughts toward her. When he then sees a message or a missed phone call from that woman, he's not going to want to get back in touch, since he knows what it means: feeling bad himself. As I said, we all walk or even run away from things that make us feel bad. Right?

When looking for a long-term relationship, a lot of men will pick the woman who makes them feel good and gives them a stable relationship without an emotional rollercoaster. They want a strong type of woman. The words often used about a successful man are: "She is the strong woman behind him, he couldn't have done it without her in his life." That's the type of woman most men look for! The kind of woman who makes him happy and makes him feel well. Only a small amount of men will choose the blonde bombshell who may or may not have any brains. You know her: the very sexy woman with the IQ of -10. Most great guys don't pick that type of woman, even when the sex obviously might be great. Even if the sex gives him a good feeling of fun, it has to be more than that. There's an important *emotional* side to this story. Please note that I'm not saying the woman should be his 'slave' that makes him feel good all the time. This book is written for YOU; I want you to feel good in the relationship. I'm sure that when you'll have a responsive man who feels good with you, you'll feel great as well. In the next chapter, I'm going to talk about the things a man finds attractive and that make him feel happy around you.

What is attractive to a man & the two types of attraction

The big question might be, "What does a man find attractive?" If you are what he finds attractive, you will have little problems with men. To understand attraction, we need to go back to the animal kingdom. We are animals. Yes, we live in houses and drive cars. We are intelligent, and most animals are not. But a big part of our brain is still the animal brain. When you are attracted to a man, it is your animal brain that is feeling and creating that attraction. The same happens in a man's brain.

In nature, the female will always look for the male who will give her nice, healthy babies so that they can have a strong opportunity and a strong possibility to survive. You, as a woman, still have the same need. Let's face it; you have to be picky as a woman. If you pick a man and you decide to make babies with that man, you're out for nine months at least. During those nine months, it is impossible to create additional babies. Then the baby is born. Is your work done then? Of course not. You have to raise the child; you have to invest a lot of your time and effort into that child. It lasts for eighteen years or more, until the child is really capable of living on its own. You have to invest a lot of time and money. That's why in your animal brain you will have to find a man who you think will give you healthy babies that will actually survive. I realize this sounds very strange, but that is what's going on in your head on a subconscious level. You have to be picky because you're out for quite a while. Nature wants you to be picky.

A man has a different mindset. If he wants to, he can impregnate a different woman every day, sometimes even multiple women per day. Men don't do those things any more because they do have responsibilities as well, we don't live in nature any longer. But if nature had its way, this would be possible. A man could have 600 or more children by the time he dies. He is not "out," so a man does not have to be picky. **That's why most men are superficial.** They only look at a woman's looks first, and if they find her attractive then they will want to have sex with her. Their subconscious minds think: "Great, let's make babies." And it works. I'm sure you've seen it; and maybe you've done it yourself.

Maybe you just used your looks to spend the night with a man. There is a little problem with this. If you use your looks to attract a man, if you wear a sexy blouse or a short skirt, or if you show your legs—a man will be attracted to you like moths to a flame. But he will be attracted for the wrong reasons. You will only create attraction in the animal side of his brain. He will want to have sex with you but the next day, he might be gone. If you look at the males in nature, you'll see they have sex with a female animal and then they leave. They don't stay around. I'm guessing that's not what you want. You want him to stay around. As a result, you'll have to create a different kind of attraction. You will find evidence that some

Keephimattracted.com

men do come back and they do stick around, but if you really analyze those situations you'll see that he only sticks around for more sex. Again, I don't think that's what you're looking for; otherwise, you wouldn't be reading this book right now.

In essence, you have to make sure that the man will commit himself to you without giving him the fear of commitment, without pushing him, or being heavy. That's very difficult. So how can you do this? When you are everything that a man is looking for, he will have no fear of commitment. If his life is more fun with you than without you, he will stick around forever. For a long-term relationship, a real relationship with a deep, emotional commitment, a man is looking for a woman with a lot of self-control. He is looking for a challenge, someone who gives him a little bit of insecurity; someone who is loyal, has integrity, physically attractive (yes, this remains important to a man), sweet, self-controlled, and stable on an emotional level.

The second important characteristic is being a challenge for your man. This means he has to work hard to get you or to keep you. Why do men love some computer games? They like to go to the next level. They have to work for it before they can get to the next step. If it's too easy, none of those men would play those games on their game console. There are women who immediately give themselves away, both on a physical and emotional level. That's not a challenge to a man.

I have met gorgeous, fun, great women who gave way too much on the first date. They made it way too easy on me, and I lost the attraction; I couldn't help it. It took me a long time before I understood why I wasn't interested anymore. If we turn it around, you'll see this concept works across both genders. Think about the men that gave themselves percent to you way too soon. They weren't a challenge for you, and you got bored.

Again, it is very important that you don't give yourself too soon on a sexual level either. If you spend the night together and have sex after the first date, there won't be any mystery anymore. He gets what he wants straight away. All the desire is gone. He is literally pleased and fulfilled. You don't give him the possibility or the chance to create that desire or dream about the fact that he wants to get closer to you, if you give it too soon. I don't know if you've seen that movie *Alfie* with the English actor, Jude Law. In the film, he says, "For every good-looking woman out there, there is a guy *tired* of banging *her*." I'm sorry for the language, but this is true. So why is that? It's because she's not a challenge any longer. Try to be a challenge both on an emotional and also a physical level.

Have you ever been to a strip club before? Maybe not, but have you ever seen something about a strip club in a movie or a television series? Do the women on the stage walk around totally naked from the start? No. They are fully dressed, and they take off each piece very slowly. They create the challenge, the mystery; they create the intrigue. It's only the physical type of desire, but it is created slowly. The emotional attraction is more difficult but important as well. You have to be a challenge on an emotional level as well.

How do you do that? Make sure that he isn't sure about your feelings toward him too soon. As you might know I coach men, and those men are quite often–100 percent of the time actually–madly in love with a certain woman. They want to know how to seduce her or how to make sure she doesn't run away. So why are they madly in love with that woman? They ask themselves questions like, "Why didn't she text me back straight away when I sent her something? She kissed me on the end of our first date, but she didn't say anything about the future. Am I going to see her again? Should I ask her out again? Is she going to say yes? She held my hand as we were walking, but then she let it go again. We are in a relationship, and today I haven't heard from her. Is there something wrong?" See what I'm talking about right here? Those guys are a little bit insecure; that's why they're asking themselves those questions. They continuously think, "I have to do stuff to seduce her." Wouldn't you want your man to think that about you?

Men are built to have those questions and even fears. They should do the work when they try to seduce you. You shouldn't. Men select; women do the choosing. A man has to seduce you and put in the effort. You as the woman have to say yes or no. It really is still that easy. This doesn't mean that you should play hard to get. Men hate that, and I'm sure you hate it as well. Let him do all the work and help him when needed. If he asks you out, you can say yes. When he texts you, you can text him back. But not right away. You see? Create a little uncertainty in his mind.

Let's say that you're on a first date with a man, and you are really pleased to be there with him. You've been looking forward to being alone with him for months and finally, it happens. If you share those feelings and thoughts with him, you take away all the challenge. He doesn't get the opportunity to wonder, "Is she having fun? Does she like me? Are we having a fun first date?" This is where you'll need to practice self-control. And I realize you probably think: "Come on, I wouldn't do that." Unfortunately, women do when they've really fallen for a man.

Think about the man who made you buy this book. Is there a certain man in your life who you like and want to understand? Are you madly in love with that man? I might be wrong, but if you're in love with him, it's probably because you wonder about some things like, "Does he love me? Can I go on with this relationship? Does it have a future?" If that's the case, then he is a challenge to you. Being a challenge creates romance. This remains important during a long-term relationship as well. He needs to understand that you will walk away the minute he shows you any disrespect. You don't need to play hard to get or become "a mysterious black box." If he's 99 percent sure that you love him and you're going to stay, that's great. He needs that 1 percent of uncertainty. Because of that small bit of insecurity, he's going to work for you. When you're in a long-term relationship with a man and you don't create a challenge there, he's 100 percent sure of you. He then knows that you are going to stay with him whatever he does or however he treats you (to a certain extent) because you love him more than anything else in the world. When that happens, he might look for that challenge elsewhere, with another woman. That's something that most women don't want to hear. You would be surprised how many people are actually looking for a challenge outside of their relationship. Men need challenges just as much as they need food. It's in their instinct, in their genes. Make sure that the challenge is in your relationship so he doesn't have to look elsewhere.

Another thing that takes challenge away mentioning your insecurities to him. I'm only talking about your insecurities toward him, not when they have something to do with your professional life, friends, etc. That's all okay. Let me give you a personal example. I love legs; that's what I look at when I feel attracted to a woman. I once had a girlfriend and, in my eyes, she had beautiful legs. I had been dating her for a couple of weeks. After a couple of weeks, all of a sudden she says, "I'm so glad we are dating, because I didn't think you would be attracted to me because I have ugly legs." I said, "What? They're not ugly!" And she said, "Yes, they are." She showed me some spots on her legs that were, indeed, not very attractive. The funny thing is, I didn't even see those imperfections before. Love had blinded me to them. I seriously thought her legs were beautiful until she showed me otherwise. All of the sudden, I would be walking around with her somewhere, see another woman with legs (yes, most of them do have them), and I thought to myself, "Now *those* are beautiful legs!" It was over; the attraction was gone just because she shared her insecurity about something between us to me. I wasn't blind anymore. I know this is ridiculous, even childish. But it happened. I know she should have been able to really be herself and share *everything* with me . . . but that's not the reality we live in. As much as I wanted to be attracted to her again, I simply wasn't any longer.

Another woman I once dated texted me after a couple of weeks. She said something like, "I'm at a certain party. I'm tired; my legs hurt. There has just been a guy who has proposed to carry me. I've said no because my legs are yours." The attraction for me rose very fast, because she created a challenge here. Other men wanted her legs as well. You see? It was very subtle, but incredibly powerful.

Attraction is a funny concept. When you have insecurities about your personality or your body, share them with your friends. Share them with everyone you want, but not with your boyfriend or husband. He doesn't need to know your personal insecurities. Don't point them out to him because he will then see them too, even when he didn't before. It's as if a guy bought a Porsche and would think, "Yes I finally own a Porsche!" The Porsche says, "Well you do realize I'm not a Ferrari, right? They have more powerful engines. They drive a little better and faster. They're more expensive. I'm sorry, but I hope you will still enjoy me . . ." Wouldn't that be weird, apart from the talking car? He knows those things; he knows his Porsche is still not a Ferrari, but he doesn't want to think about that. Don't tell him. You might feel the urge to share your insecurities with him. That way, if he stays, you're really sure that he wants you for you. That's true, but why take that risk? Try to not talk about your personal imperfections. He'll notice them when he does in due time. Everyone has imperfections, and that is good. So it's quite important to have a lot of self-confidence. This is very attractive to a man. There are women with a lot of imperfections but are more attractive to men because of their self-confidence than beautiful women with no self-confidence whatsoever.

Insecurity can be created by not always talking about the feelings you have for him. Let's say that you're dating a guy. You go out with him; you do fun stuff with him, so in essence he knows that you like him. But if you don't talk about it, he doesn't know how *much* you like him and that leaves a little bit of room for insecurity.

I've seen some naturals who actually play games with men. They might kiss a man and then all of a sudden they turn off all signs and signals of interest after that. The man is left in the dark, wondering "What? She just kissed me, but now she's behaving distant. What is this?" It makes him crazy, and they end up falling very hard because his natural instinct to chase her awakens especially since he had gotten something from her first. You see? It's as if you take the lollipop away from a child; it really wants it back.

Men love insecurity, even when most men will not admit this when asked. That's why they play games like poker. Men find it fun because they all sit around a table and everyone has a couple of cards. There's money on the table. As a man sits there, he can see the face of his opponents around him. He can see their eyes, their body language and he will try to "read" them to know whether they have good cards or not. There's insecurity. "Does he have better cards than me? Will he take my money?" And that's nice! Men like to chase after those things. This will motivate them to *make it certain, to remove the insecurity and make it secure.* You might conclude that when you take all the insecurity away and give him the thing he's looking for (security), he'll be happy. No. If you give him what he wants, the chase is over! And then he will have to chase something else, or someone else, to get the same feeling, that same adrenaline rush back.

Another characteristic of a woman most men find emotionally attractive is loyalty. If you start to flirt with other men and he sees it or knows it, then in the beginning he's going to fight harder for you. He's going the think, "She's mine!" and "I want her!" You are going to get an initial reaction of love from him, but he doesn't *like* it. In the long term, he will never stay with a woman who is not loyal to him in one form or another.

An attractive woman is also someone who is physically attractive. This remains important, but is less important than most women think. When he's attracted to you after meeting you, it's the physical attractiveness that plays a role. If you want to be in a long-term relationship with a man, the physical looks are less important. So what's physically attractive to a man? Most men like breasts; other men look at your legs; others only care about your face, etc. So this is different for every guy. Whoever you are, whatever you look like, there will always be men that are attracted to what you look like.

The easiest way to create attraction is using your smile. A woman who smiles to a man actually shows a lot of self-confidence. Try it. When you're walking outside, simply smile to the men that you see. Be aware, because they might come over and talk to you. They will become much more responsive. Men want to have fun; men want to feel good when they are around you. When you smile often, you communicate "fun."

Women who can keep the attraction alive in the long term know when to be sweet. So, what does this mean exactly? Well, people who are sweet all the time, finish last. I'm sure you know that "nice guys finish last," and the same happens to a woman. People take advantage of people who are too nice and cannot say "no." Being the opposite, being a bad boy or a bad girl, is not so cool either. Naturals know how to play the sweetness card and when to use it . . . they are sweet when they have to be. They are sweet, for instance, when the man is trying to seduce them, and when they obviously like the man as well. They help the man without playing hard to get, but they still allow him to chase. Let's say that the guy you like asks you out on a first date, and you see that he's very nervous. You're happy that he's asking you out on a date, and say yes with a smile. Don't play hard to get then, however, don't be too nice, (e.g. "Oh John, I thought you'd never ask! I've been dreaming about this for weeks now"), as I'm sure you know.

And the final important part that makes a woman attractive, especially in the long term, is when she is emotionally stable. This type of stability is closely related to the self-control issues I already discussed. Women who are uptight are unattractive. Women who get mad or jealous easily won't create lasting attraction either. Men want emotional stability. So, have an honest look at yourself right now and see if you are emotionally stable toward the man in your life. How is your emotional character? Are you the kind of woman who is very happy one day and very depressed the next? Make sure that you emit the right signal to the men in your life, especially to the one who you want to attract and keep.

Making sure he picks YOU and stays with you

How can you be different than other women? How can you make sure that the man will pick you and not another woman? How can you become more attractive than other women, especially in a long-term relationship? I'm not talking about putting five women in a row and making sure he picks you based on your looks. If he would have five dates with each of those other women and yourself, how can you be sure that he would pick you and that he feels the most attraction toward you?

Obviously, you have to do all of the things I've been already discussed and all the things I will discuss in the rest of this book. There is, however, one thing that really stands out. The one thing you have to show, the one thing you have to portray is self-control. If you show that type of characteristic, then you will be worth more than any other woman in his life. Yes, here it is yet again! It's being able to control your own emotions in different types of situations. A woman with a lot of self-control is very attractive to a man. He can see that you have self-control by studying a couple of your characteristics and seeing how you react to certain things and in particular situations. Are you a positive person, or are you a negative person? How do you feel about yourself? Do you have a lot of self-confidence or a low level of self-confidence? How do you react to difficult emotional situations in your life? Are you a jealous type of woman? Is it easy to make you mad? Is it easy to frustrate you or not? The ideal version of a woman, for a man, is a woman who always has a smile on her face, who is always happy, and gives a lot of value to his life.

I know this ideal woman doesn't exist. You don't need to be perfect; you simply need to give him a lot of emotional value. As I've said before, if life is more fun with you than without you, he will never ever walk away. I know it's impossible to be this idealized version with a constant smile on your face, but what type of energy do you emit when you are amongst other men or with your guy? It is that energy that can push them away or draw them in. *That's actually all you have to do to keep him attracted.* Give him the right type of feeling when he's around you. If he feels this energy, he will be sucked toward you and he won't walk away ever. Obviously we do live in the real world and the sun doesn't shine every day, but we all must strive for an emotional balance. When you're around someone who emits more negative energy than positive, you won't want to stick around for too long.

It's a big stereotype, but if you think about what men dislike about women, there's one thing that always pops out: "She nags." I'm sure you've heard this. Men joke about it on some sitcoms and in movies. *According to Jim*, a TV sitcom, with Jim Belushi features a couple: Jim and Cheryl. Jim is a sweet macho man with a lot of male energy and male habits. Cheryl is a sweet housewife. Jim and Cheryl are complete opposites. Since Cheryl is a woman; her female energy is very big. Jim is a real man; he doesn't want to talk about emotions.

79

He only wants to watch his favorite football team, drink beers, and eat a lot. Because of those differences, they really love each other, and they form a great team. The show is all about the stereotypes in this show and that's great because we can learn from it.

Let's go back to self-control. How do you respond to different things that happen in your life? What are your emotions? What are the things that you say to yourself when something good or bad happens around you? It's getting a little bit more complex right now, but the things you say to yourself will define your emotions.

I will never ever forget this, many years ago I was in California and there had been some major fires. A lot of houses were simply gone. There was a news crew that was following a woman who would see the remains of her house again for the very first time. They walked up the hill where her house was supposed to be, but it was gone. The fire had destroyed everything.

The camera crew followed her. They saw this big pile of melted metal. The interviewer said, "What was this?" "This was my collection of antique cars," said the owner, "they were not insured." Most people would be crying at that point, because they just lost everything. But she didn't cry. The interviewer was a little bit dazzled by this. He said, "What are you going to do? Why aren't you crying?" And that emotionally strong woman replied, "If I cry . . . is that going to solve any of my problems? No. Will that bring my house and my cars back? No. I have to see this as an opportunity to start over again. I have a decision to make right now. I can cry and feel down for the rest of my life, or I can say 'Shit happens, and I'm going to continue.'" Wow! Can you imagine how much better she is feeling since she uses this kind of self-talk? This is not a kind of motivational guru book here, but I hope you see the importance of how you talk to yourself.

Bad things happen to you as well, some small, some big. How do you react? What are the stories you tell yourself? Those define your emotions. A good example I always use during my coaching sessions is the following: Let's say Brad and Bob are both American soldiers. They are in a dangerous country and at the same time, they both step on a land mine. The mine explodes and they both lose one leg. Something very bad just happened and they will need to tell themselves a story. Brad says: "Why did this happen to me? Of all of the directions I could have chosen, why did I choose to walk right onto that mine? My life is over . . .". Brad will lead a sad life and will emit a lot of negative energy because he chose negative self-dialogue. Brad will not like himself and his life; and other people won't love to be around Brad. Bob, who has lost a leg as well, uses a different type of self-dialogue when he thinks: "My God, have I been lucky. I could have been killed; I could have lost BOTH legs. I can still walk with a fake leg or crutches. Boy am I lucky!" Bob will have a great life, he will be grateful, have lots of friends and attract people because of his positive outlook on life. Both had the same life changing event, both had a different reaction to it and *that* defines the life they will live and the feelings they'll feel on a daily basis.

There are many possible land mines in relationships as well and it's important to monitor how you talk to yourself about them. Suppose that you have a date set up with a man. Maybe it's just a first date, maybe you've been dating for months already, but the guy in this story shows up fifteen minutes late. What are you going to say to yourself when you see this is happening? Maybe you say things like, "What a jerk! This always happens to me. Am I not pretty enough? Is there something wrong with me? I don't deserve this . . ." Obviously if you say things like that, you are going to be uptight. When he finally arrives, the entire atmosphere, the energy of the date, is going to be ruined. It is very unlikely that he is going to have fun. Maybe you're the type of woman who says, "Maybe there was a traffic jam or something. Maybe he was working late. Maybe he was in a meeting and he couldn't get out sooner. I don't care, I'll just wait." If you say things like this and he finally arrives, you are going to be happy. It will probably be a fun date; everything is going to be cool. The atmosphere of the date is going to be fun. Do you see the difference? I specifically said fifteen minutes late, since you should of course always demand respect from a man and never allow a man to treat you as if you're not that important to him.

Even when you have a long-term relationship, how do you respond to the things that happen in that relationship?

What are the things you say to yourself at that time? Are they making you feel mad, or are they making you feel happy? By the way, don't worry if you talk negatively to yourself in those moments. I've done that plenty of times, we all do that. I've even ruined a lot of my relationships earlier on in life simply because of this. Every time a woman did something wrong, I would start to get mad. I would say things to myself like, "See? She doesn't love me." I would get uptight. No one woman is attracted to that, of course, so all of those relationships were quickly over. If I had used some self-control, I would have said to myself, "Okay she just did something that I don't really like, but if I'm going to be uptight about this right now then I'm going to ruin the relationship. I'm going to ruin the energy that we have between us. Is what she did worth that?" If she really did something wrong, something that I don't like, I'm simply going to say it and then let it go. I'm not going to get mad; I'm not going to be uptight. I'm not going to give her the silent treatment. All of those things don't work, of course. They actually show that you don't have any self-control. When you have a lot of self-control, you know how to control your own emotions.

Let's do a little test. Is there a mirror you can go to right now? If there is a mirror, position yourself in front of that mirror. Make sure that you can see yourself. If you can't, simply read this and then go try it. Position yourself in front of the mirror and look at yourself in a sad way. Look at yourself as if your goldfish . See how you feel when you look at your own sad face. Then put a smile on your face, the biggest possible smile you can show. Look at yourself like that and focus on your eyes. Think of how your cat accidentally filled in the right lottery numbers for you, and you've won the lottery because of this! How do you feel right now? You feel different than you did looking at your sad face, don't you? Guess what? There's only one thing that changed: the way you were looking at yourself. That's the funny part. Your emotions don't just influence other people, they influence YOU as well. If you are positive, if you are full of self-confidence, energy, fun–people who see you will get a little bit of that feeling. They will be attracted to and by you. They will love to be around you because they get energized. If you did the exercise in front of the mirror, you've felt it. As you're reading this, please force a smile on your face and count to 10 while you keep a full smile. Please, don't just continue reading. Hold on, smile and keep that smile for 10 seconds. Can you feel how your emotions are changing? It's all about the energy you emit.

The opposite is true as well. When you are negative with no self-confidence, if you feel sad or ugly, people around you are going to feel that as well. It's a self-fulfilling prophecy. Most people are not going to like to be around you. Do you have a friend who always nags and always talks about the stuff that isn't working out in life? He or she says, "You want to know what happened today? She still didn't call me back. This and that went wrong." Do you like to be around people like that? Of course not! You need to monitor the type of energy that you are emitting to the people around you as well. This is especially important if you are the type of person who thinks: "I should be able to be myself. If I am sad, if I am depressed, I should be able to show this to my friends, to my partner, and so on. They should take me as I am." You're right, they will for a couple of weeks and then they will be gone. They won't call you that often anymore. I'm not just talking about dates or relationships here; I'm even talking about simple friendships. It shouldn't be that way, as the saying goes, "through good and bad times" . . . but in most cases, people won't love being around you if you're negative. That's life, and we need to face up to this reality to get the most out of it.

When you are happy, even if you fake it, people around you are going to be happy. That, in turn, is going to make you happy. It's an upward spiral. That's why self-control is so important. If there is something wrong in the relationship, if there is something wrong in your life and you feel emotionally beat down by that–do not show it right away. Think about the consequences first.

It is not the goal that you are his slave and he can do whatever he wants without you saying anything about it. You deserve lots of respect, affection, and love. You can talk about it, but don't show the emotions. That's the big point to remember. For instance: you've been waiting for your date. Your date arrives thirty minutes late. That is simply not done. That's not a sign of respect. If you showed your emotions, you would be sad, mad, or hurt. A natural, however, would say, "Hi. How was your day? Were you in a traffic jam?" And then she would say with a smile on her face, "You know you can only do this to me once. Next time I won't be here anymore. So what's up? How was your day?" She continues the conversation. See? She stated her opinion in a way full of self-confidence and in a very assertive way. She demanded respect. Nevertheless, she did not lose her self-control; she never showed any emotions and remained emotionally stable. Men cannot help it and are very attracted to this type of behavior. I'm sure the date will still be fun, and I'm also sure the guy won't do this to her twice. Do you see the difference? Being mad, sad, hurt, and revealing those emotions: "Why were you late, don't you like me? Where is this going? Do we have a future?" turns the man off. Demanding respect without showing emotions: "Hey, you were really late. I've been waiting for 30 minutes and that's OK, but it's the only time I'll ever do this so you've just used up your one credit (say this with a smile). So, how was your day?" This is a very powerful way to assert yourself, get what you want from him or you'll walk away. He knows that and if he's attracted, even a little bit, his interest in you will rise! If not and he does do it again, you can say "so long." It's best to never ever let a man treat you without respect and when he stands you up twice, he's not what you deserve. He won't change anyway.

There's another interesting fact that Daniel Goleman taught me about emotions. Emotions are addictive, and we all want other people to make us feel good. When you want to get a certain emotion from someone, you need to show it first and then you might get that same emotion back in return. If you are mad at someone and start to yell, that person will probably be mad at you in return, right? When you are driving your car and someone upsets you and you show your middle finger, then the other person is going to get mad as well. You are going to get back what you give. You should try this as a test: when you are driving your car and somebody else is mad at you and shows you the finger or honks their horn. Instead of getting mad yourself, smile and pretend you're sorry. This is counterintuitive. You'll see that the other person's face will change immediately. In most cases, you'll take the anger away. Show the emotion you'd like to get back from other people. Be the first to start it. When it comes to your man or boyfriend, when you are happy and upbeat during the day, he will be too. If you're loving toward him, he will be loving toward you.

A great tool to deal with men is to try and understand them, to see a situation through their eyes. I'm sure you would like to be understood by the man in your life. Well, if you start to understand him, it will be easier for him to see it from your perspective as well. Let's say he does something wrong. He doesn't give you enough attention or love, he's too late for a date, he doesn't text you back, etc.; it seems like he's not interested anymore. You get uptight because of this, it changes your mood. It's possible that he *is* losing interest, but that's not the only possibility. He may have a lot of problems at work, for instance. If that's true and you are upset, he is going to think that you really don't get him. Because of this, being around you will not be as fun as it used to be, and his interest in you will start to gradually decline. If, however, you would say to him, "Hey, it hurts me, but I understand. I can see that you have a lot of stuff to do at work. It's okay." That's what a natural would say. It will take down his defenses and force him on a subconscious level to analyze his own behavior. He is going to have the freedom to say, "Actually, I get it. I am spending too much time at work. I should give her more attention, she deserves it." The differences are, in fact, very, very subtle, but the outcome is very, very different. In the second example, he's not forced to change; he's changed from the inside out. He thinks HE decided it for himself. When a woman pushes a man into doing anything, it can backfire. When she uses a strategy where he has the freedom to realize he's wrong, like the example I explained above, the outcome will be better.

Take a second, if you can, to think about what I just explained. Think about your past relationships and problems with men. If you had acted differently, like a natural would have, would the outcome have been different? As I said before, sometimes the man really is a jerk. Sometimes he really doesn't love you and when that's the case, nothing you do will change the outcome. But they're not all jerks. All the other ones actually have a legitimate excuse for something they are doing wrong toward you. If you take the time to understand what that real reason is, when you explain to him that you actually understand it but you don't like it, sometimes the situation turns out differently. In the next chapter, I'm going to talk about how you can change a man. Or is that not a good idea?

How to change a man

So, here we are. This is a subject women have been trying to figure out for ages, decades, and centuries: how to change a man. I've been coaching women for several years now. Every single woman I coached on a private basis asked me, "So how do I change him?" Well, I have news for you: you can't. It's impossible to change a man. A man might tell a woman he has changed his ways. He might seem to have changed, but he would only be fooling her and maybe even himself.

A client I had a couple of years ago had a big problem. Her fiancé had some kind of addiction, and she didn't like it at all. It was a deal breaker for her. She made him promise that he would really stop that behavior before they would get married. She said, "I don't want to marry you if you still do that." He said, "Hey, I've changed. I don't do that anymore. I've changed. I won't ever do it again." They get married, and they live happily ever after. Or do they? Two years in the marriage, she finds out he never stopped doing what he promised to never do again. She thought he had changed. He had been fooling her all that time. Apparently their entire marriage was a big lie and needless to say, she was very heartbroken. So she wanted me to teach her how to change him. I had to make it very clear to her that you cannot change another person. It's impossible to change anyone else, but yourself. It's best not to even try it, because you are wasting your time. You will get hurt in the end. People can only change themselves. They have to want it for themselves; it will not work if they do it "for you."

Everyone has flaws. When you enter into a relationship with a man, you have to really think about, "Do I accept his flaws? Yes or no? Are they deal-breakers? Yes or no?" If they are, please don't try to change him. Walk away, even if it hurts.

There is one golden rule when it comes to men: You will always get the man you've picked. A lot of women tell me, "He never actually tells me that he loves me. He never gives me any signs of romantic interest." That's what they want from their man. Then I say, "Well think about the men who actually gave you all of that." Usually they then respond, "Oh well I lost interest in those men." Most people want something they can't really have. Some things that you really don't like about your man are actually the things that are attractive to you. You might *need* them to love him and feel attraction. It, however, is important to assess the situation. When his differences or behavior really hurt your feelings all the time, it might be worth dropping this relationship. Don't try to be that woman who wastes all her energy on a guy, only to find out later that everything was a lie. That hurts even more than walking away right now.

Men and their Emotions (do they even have any?)

I'm going to cover men and their emotions in this chapter. I might be wrong, but I think that most of the problems you have with men come down to men not being able to show their emotions and sometimes not even being able to have emotions at all. For men, an emotion is something strange. It gives them an uncomfortable feeling. What I'm about to talk about in this chapter is going to sound crazy to you as a woman. You, of course, love emotions. Men really don't.

When you give a man bad emotions, if you make him feel emotions that he doesn't really love to feel, he might turn off a switch in his head. All of a sudden, he is going to change his behavior toward you. He's going to "need some space," or sometimes even run away. Have you ever seen a man do this? On an emotional level, a man is totally different than a woman. You can, for instance, see this in a professional environment. When you look at men at work, most of them are loners. When they climb the corporate ladder, they try to do it all alone. When you see women in the professional world, you'll see that most of them have a lot of friends in the work place. They love to have lunch together, discuss office gossip, and talk. When they arrive at work, they might say to a colleague, "Oh that's a nice purse! Where did you get it?"

They make sure they have social connections with other people.

When you work around any major city during lunch hour, you should see more men than women eating alone. They really don't care. They don't *need* other people. They don't need those discussions and emotions as much as women do. That's a big difference between men and women already.

When you have conversations with your girlfriends, most of the topics you discuss will be "emotional," they'll be about how you feel about something. Men don't do this. They do not talk about their emotions. They talk about money, women, sports, and other hobbies. That's a stereotype. It is only a stereotype because it's true. Because of our society where men and women are equal, we think that both sexes are the same. That, in my humble opinion, is a big, big mistake. Of course they should be equal, but they are not the same. This idea created a lot of problems in relationships. All of a sudden, women became very powerful, and there was a whole range of men who decided that the woman is the stronger sex on the planet. Some men thought, "What I have to do to seduce her is really give her everything that she needs. I have to be nice to her; I have to be sweet. I have to buy her flowers. I have to show her that I love her. I have to treat her well." These men then overdo this. I'm sure you've met men like these. They are the nice guys you can't really fall for or stay in love with because you simply walk over them. They don't believe that men and women are equal; they believe women are more than men, that you, the woman, are the queen of their world. That isn't very attractive to most women.

Women make the same mistake sometimes. They think, "Men and women are equal, so they are the same." In my private coaching sessions, I had a lot of women who made little mistakes like this. For instance, they sent a romantic card with a sweet message to a man. Most women would love to receive a romantic card . . . men, however, do not know how to respond or react when they get one. That romantic gesture gives him emotions that he's never felt before.

Because of our society, we sometimes forget that we are still animals, beasts. That's what we are on a subconscious level. Why we do the things that we do is mostly defined by our animal instincts. We crave food; we crave attention; we crave love; we crave sex and reproduction. That has never ever changed. We still have all of those needs and wants. Centuries ago, when we were cavemen and cavewomen, times were different. The man had the role of the leader. He was the boss of the family, even of the village. He had to make sure that there was food on the table. He had to make sure the village was well defended and the family was taken care of. He needed to protect the women and children and give them food and shelter. If he didn't do his job, the entire family would die. The woman had to take care of the babies and raise the children so that they could become great women or good, strong men. This was a perfect balance. It was team work, and both sexes used their strengths. This is still embedded in our instincts and subconscious mind; it's still in our genes. Most families were still living like this up until the sixties. The woman took care of the house and the children, and the man made sure there was enough money for the family to survive.

Most women start thinking about kids at a certain age. Why is that? It's your instinct; it's your body telling you that you should create offspring. As a woman, you are programmed to care for something, whereas a man wants to fight or defend something. In nature, males will fight other males to find a female. Although we are supposed to be civilized now and different than our ancestors, most of our instincts and natural programming are still the same. When you as a woman want your man to share his emotions ("C'mon, you can be yourself! Talk about this! Men these days they cry as well."), then you are going against his nature. At first, he might do these things simply to please you, but he's not going to feel right. And he will be more and more turned off by what he will be feeling.

In one of the episodes of the sitcom *Friends,* Bruce Willis plays a cameo role as Rachel's boyfriend. There's a funny scene where Bruce plays a strong masculine man. Rachel is trying to open him up so he can share his emotions. They're sitting on the couch in Joey's apartment, and she really wants him to open up. She says, "C'mon talk about your emotions. Talk about your past. You can really do this." And all of a sudden, she opens Pandora's box. It's a parody of the real situation. He starts to cry and talk about his mom and how he didn't get any love, etc. Rachel doesn't know how to respond to this because it's not attractive at all. It's the thing she wanted, but the minute she gets it, there's no attraction anymore. It feels wrong even to her. For relationships to really work well, men need to be men, and women need to be women. The differences are very important. Those opposites between men and women attract!

When problems arise in the Relationship

What happens when you have problems in your relationship? Where does it go wrong and why does it happen? I've read a lot of books written by Geoffrey Miller. Geoffrey Miller is a biologist who has been studying attraction, how or why we do things in relationships, how we select our sexual partners, etc. He wrote a book called *The Mating Mind*; it's a very interesting book about sexual attraction and why we select someone over other people. He also wrote a book called *Spent*. That book deals with why we buy certain things to seduce the other sex. According to him, most of the things we buy are bought because we want to seduce the other sex. Why do men by a flashy, fast car? Is it possible that he buys one to be significant? Why does he want to be significant? Maybe it's to attract women? Of course! There's nothing wrong with that. What are the things that you buy to attract men or to be more significant? Most women buy pretty clothes and shoes so they can look good and attract men.

Some feminists will say, "Well I don't buy *anything* for men. I buy it for me." Why would they buy it for themselves? Maybe it's to feel better. Maybe it's because they want the significance, they want the attention when they walk into a room the men look at them and that makes them feel empowered. Or maybe they just want to look better than other women. Even that will be so men would notice them and not the other women. Some women might consciously realize this, but in essence, our purchases are often made to impress or attract the other sex.

In the animal kingdom, the males fight each other. The female then picks the strongest male, the one that still survives or that didn't give up. When you look at lions, it's the strongest male that gets the best females. That's great for the strongest male, and that's great for the female lions as well. The lionesses get access to the strongest genes; their offspring will have the best chances of survival. Some animals will actually fight for that dominance. Others have different systems. A peacock for instance has a flashy, big tail. Over the centuries, the female peacock has always selected the male peacock by eyes on his tail over the peacock with a less flashy tail. Those who did not have an eye on their tails wouldn't get any sex, so they couldn't reproduce. They are now extinct. The ones with an eye on their tails survived. Over the years, the eyes on the peacocks' tails have always become bigger and bigger and bigger. Why does a female peacock pick a male peacock with a big eye on a big tail? It tells her something about that male peacock. You are probably going to feel attraction toward the men where your subconscious body radar says: "Good genes, reproduce with this guy." If your body thinks, "With that man, I can make great-looking babies, healthy babies that are going to survive and will be capable of making babies for themselves" then you are going to feel attraction toward that man. This mostly happens on a subconscious level. You have to look at different characteristics of a man to see if he has good genes, right? You don't do this by thinking about it and going over all of his positive aspects so you can consciously decide: "Yeah, I should be attracted to him."

This is not a conscious process, it happens automatically. For the female peacocks, they look at the eye on the big tail for a certain reason. Just imagine that you are a male peacock, and you're walking in the woods with a big tail and a flashy eye. Those eyes draw a lot of attention to the peacock. It's hard to miss it. The tails are so big that most peacocks can't even fly anymore. It shouldn't be too hard to catch and eat one of those peacocks for a fox or any other predator. So the male peacocks that you do find in their natural habitat must be smart, really smart. They outsmarted the foxes and other predators that try to hunt them down and eat them for dinner. That male peacock has so many disabilities, so many physical disadvantages (flashy tail, not being able to fly away when being hunted), and he still survives. "That must surely be one with great genes, with great survival skills," the female peacock thinks. And she's right! You, as a woman, do the same thing on an unconscious level. You are constantly sizing up men to see if they fit your needs. Part of this is a conscience process, but most of it isn't. When you talk to a man, and the man says, "I'm a janitor" then he would lose points. If he says, "I'm a janitor, but four months a year I travel to war areas in Africa to find mines in minefields and I help create a safer environment for the children there" then he gains points. Am I right?

In nature, male animals have to prove themselves toward the female animals by fighting or showing some signal that proves they have good genes. **So females are in control!** You have the male lions fighting to get 'access' to the lionesses; you have the peacocks trying to create the biggest eye on their tail, taking a big risk to being eaten, just to get a female partner. Does this mean the woman has all the power at all times then? Not really. The male lion has to decide a certain female is worth fighting for. The male animal sees the female animal and says, "That's the one. She's worth it." Then and only then will he put in an effort to make her say yes, to win her over. **Men do the picking; women do the choosing.** It's like that in the animal kingdom, and it's like that in our human world as well. Please write this bold sentence down somewhere, it will help you with men. Choose the men who have picked you first, who are willing to fight for you!

We are part of nature, we are 'animals' ourselves. This entire system still applies to us, too. Some men think women have it easy. A woman walks into a bar; she stands there by herself without a drink. If it's an attractive woman, and all of a sudden, there are men who come over to talk to her and offer her drinks. Must be easy, right? Men dream about this. They think, "How great would it be if I simply walk into a bar and have these women simply walking up to me and asking me out and buying me a drink?" This is what men *think* they want. Nevertheless, as with everything else, once he gets it, he doesn't want it anymore.

This creates problems nowadays. Some women start to seduce men and take matters into their own hands. They start to flirt. They start to seek his approval. They want to be picked by him, so they dress sexy or they start to dance in front of him. That's still okay. Some women, however, take it one step further, and they start to do the "picking" themselves. Remember: Men do the picking; women do the choosing. If you find a woman who does the picking herself, she quite often creates challenges and problems should there ever be a relationship with that specific guy. Those women see a man and they think, "I want a relationship with that guy. He's a cute, so I'm going to walk up to him. We live in a society these days where men and women are equal. I am allowed do this; I go for what I want." This is where the problem starts. If you know women who do this, you will see that they often don't have successful long-term relationships. The man might like this at first. If the woman is really attractive, he might think: "Wow, I don't even have to do anything." But after a couple of dates, it just doesn't feel natural to him and he starts to lose interest without even understanding why. If the woman in question isn't that attractive, nothing will happen, men will see her as 'needy' from the get go.

I realize you might not like the theory I'm trying to explain here. You might even be offended by it, but please, stay with me since I'm trying to tell it like it is in the real world and help you. Remember my story about nature? The women have the choice. The female has the choice; she says yes or no. **She's however only supposed to say yes or no to the men who have picked her, chosen her, and want to seduce her.** Those lions, those men, have already made the decision on their own. They've already said, "That's the one. That's the woman with whom I want to spend the rest of my life." They won't find it difficult to have a big, emotional connection with you, to have a great future with you, and to take every next step in the relationship. You know why? It's because they have picked you first. Men who risk getting rejected by you, really want you. They are willing to get hurt to get you. It will be a lot easier to have an emotionally stable relationship with those men from the get go, since you are aligned with nature, with the way things are supposed to happen.

"The way nature intended it to happen" has changed ever since women became emancipated and started "picking" the men themselves. This might work sometimes, but when you look at relationships that started this way, most of them won't survive. The man will lose interest.

In nature, the woman has the strongest position. She can do the choosing; she has the power of "yes" or "no." She has men who want her, and she selects whom *she* wants to be with. In nature, the man is eager to find out if the woman is going to say "yes" or "no," whether she is going to choose him over another man. That's how it's supposed to be. You'll see men stay in love as long as they feel insecure, as long as they have to continue chasing you. Some women can maintain this situation for the entire long-term relationship. The man always feels he has to continue to be worthy of her.

Do you see what's emerging right here? Is this something you've seen in your own life? The women who switched and chose men who haven't shown interest in them *first*. They try to do the picking themselves whereas nature dictates: Men do the picking, women do the choosing. What happens here is that those women will feel really insecure about the feelings of that specific man. That's because they indeed do not know IF the man was and is interested. On top of that, those men will quickly lose interest even if they were interested, because they weren't allowed to fight for her, to chase her. There was no challenge.

I'm sure you know this feeling: you're out on a first date with a man; the connection feels great to you. You really like him. You start to think about the future a little bit, about how it would be to have a relationship with that man. Maybe you think: "I like him, and so he must like me, too. I like him, so he has to be the right guy. Right? He should feel the same."

It's hard to really know it since most real men won't talk about their feelings right away, and if *he* didn't pick you, there's no way to tell whether he's really in to you or not.

If you look at your girlfriends, when you look at your own past you might see that a man needs more time to make a strong, emotional decision about the next steps of the relationship. Most men need time to think about this. So-called "nice guys" don't, but I'm sure you're not really attracted to those types of men as we have already discussed in previous chapters. Now if you are in a relationship or in the dating stage with a man who didn't really pick you because *you* seduced him, then he will need a lot more time to make those types of decisions. Even if you look like a supermodel, it doesn't matter because you're going against nature's laws. Let me repeat. It's easy to seduce a man; it's easy to get him to have sex you. It's quite hard to get him to step into a long-term relationship with you, **especially if he did not pick you first.**

When you look at the lives around you and your own life, you'll see that the men who have picked a woman *first* (so the man approached the woman first) are most likely to stay in a long-term relationship with her. The only exception to that rule are the players, the guys who really only want a one-night stand and are not interested in you as a human being. We're not going to talk too much about those types of men, because you deserve a lot better.

Here's how it worked until the late seventies: a man meets a woman; the man feels attraction. Maybe the woman feels attraction too, but she doesn't show it yet. The man feels attraction, and he shows it. The woman smiles, thus she shows that she's actually open to the man. She gave a little "Okay, you can come and talk to me" sign. That's all she has to do. The man did the picking when he started the seduction process; the woman did the choosing by allowing him to do so. The man walks up to the woman, and they start a conversation. The woman then starts an unconscious form of a job interview and starts to test the man to see if he meets her expectations. She wants to know if he's funny, what kind of job he has, and what his life is like. She needs to decide if this is the type of man with whom she wants to make babies, on an unconscious level, of course. She wonders, "Is this the type of man I want to spend the rest of my life with? Is this the type of man who is going to take care of me and not run away? Will he be a good father?" Because of that conversation, the woman is going to choose whether or not she wants to see him again. *She* has the power in this story. This is what happened since we evolved from the apes. We still have this system programmed in ourselves because this is how "seduction" functions in nature.

All of a sudden, women had the emancipation and equality rights, and the big mistake, in my opinion, is that most people thought that women and men were the same. The entire society started to change. During the eighties, most women took on a job as well. They no longer needed a man for financial security. They could survive on their own; they could even raise kids on their own. They pushed the man out of his natural position. They took charge. This was the right thing to do. It was as if a woman wasn't worth as much as a man before this emancipation. In relationships, however, this made her give away her powers. Previously, men did the picking (and took the risk of getting hurt), women did the choosing. She had all the power and she gave away her power by starting to seduce men and show interest. The entire natural system got screwed up. Both parties, men and women, are in trouble right now.

As a man, I like Porsches. But why do men like Porsches? They give them significance. That's not all; they also like that car because they have to work hard to get a Porsche. Men have to save a lot of money. They have to walk into the dealership and talk to the salesman. Then they have to wait a couple of weeks before they can get their Porsche. So at night, they still have to look at the poster they pinned on their wall, and then finally they can go get it. That's the way it's supposed to be. It shouldn't be easy!

Picture the average man right now. He's home, watching TV with a bag of chips on his lap, and all of a sudden, his doorbell rings. He opens the door and there's the guy from the Porsche dealership. The salesman says, "Here are the keys to your Porsche." "But I didn't order a Porsche," says the man. "I know, but it's for you for free. Here you go. Have fun with it!" the salesman says. At first, ten days for instance, the guy would jump up and down every day with a big smile, since he'll be as happy as a child. He just got a Porsche, his dream! But something is wrong. The chase wasn't there. It wouldn't feel right. He wouldn't enjoy driving that car as much as he should and before long, he would start dreaming about an even better car. Why is this? It's because it was *so* easy he thinks he can do even better. Does that sound familiar to you?

If you look at the research that studied people who actually won the lottery and won multiple millions of dollars, you'll see that all of those people become depressed. And five to ten years later, they're bankrupt. They've lost all their money, all their friends, etc. If you don't have to work for things, you don't know what the value of it is. This is true for women, but especially for men who need that chase, that hard work to feel proud of what they've achieved, to feel significant.

Up until the 80s, a man really had to work hard to get a woman to like him. He knew the value. He had to fight for it; he had to do a lot. Right now we're in an era where the man doesn't need to try hard. Some women all of the sudden start to seduce him, fight for his attention, ask him things like, "Do you love me?" The rule here is that you have to make sure that he still has to work for your attention, to keep you in his life and not the other way around.

Did you ever buy something that wasn't easy to buy? Something that you had to work for, save money for, and wait for and finally you've got it? Do you own something like that? How did "getting it" feel? Quite good, right? It's even better than receiving something of higher financial value that you didn't work for. I'm pretty sure that you're bored of it after a couple of weeks. It's the same in relationships. If you have to work for it, you stay in love; the excitement stays a lot longer. That, by the way, is probably why you're reading this book. You're probably in love with a man who you have to work for, right?

It would be better if we could turn back the clock to before the eighties, relationship wise. Right now we have men who don't walk up to women any more. They don't seduce women; they don't talk to them because a) they are too afraid, or b) they think, "I don't even have to do it anymore. The women who are really interested in me will walk up to me." Then you have those men who indeed do talk about their emotions because they read in *Men's Health* magazine that women like it when men show their feelings. They, however, wonder why they never get to the second date. They don't know what they did wrong. They had the first date; they gave thirty-seven compliments; they talked about how happy they were to be there and how much they would like to see her again. They don't understand why she loses interest because of that. Other men are in love with a woman, but they don't know how to seduce women anymore. One of their girlfriends told them, "Just explain to her how you feel. Just show her how you feel. Talk about it. She can say yes or she can say no. You already have the no, you might get the yes." That's what those men are advised. So those men go out with a girl they like, and they talk about their emotions. They tell her, "I love you and I've loved you all my life. I just wanted to share my feelings with you."

Did you ever feel lasting attraction for a man who was that generous with his feelings during the first date? Most women lose the attraction. The man in this case forgot how to seduce the woman first. He didn't create any feelings of love. He forgot to flirt and create attraction. He thought, "I like her, so she must like me too, right?" No, that's not how it works.

Women make mistakes as well. You have women who start to seduce men. So, *they* pick a man. They do the seducing, the approaching, they go in for the first kiss, etc. This might seem to work at first. Nevertheless, these women are forgetting a couple of crucial steps. All of this simply feels very strange to a man. He might start a relationship with a woman who seduced *him* first but there comes a point where she's wondering where this is going, where she's ready for the next step . . . and he isn't. She did the picking instead of him; she's a couple of steps ahead.

What you should remember is that the more you follow nature's rulebook, the more success you will have with men. You can create deep, emotional connections with men. You can create relationships where you don't have to worry where the relationship is going. Sometimes there will be a couple of discussions and maybe even a fight here and there. The sun can't shine every single day, but you won't have that feeling of insecurity if you let nature do its work.

You don't need to be perfect either. You can take the lead here and there as well. Let me give you an example. Say that you walk into a bar and you see a great guy. For one reason or another you say, "I'm not going to listen to nature. I will take the first step. I will smile, and I will go talk to him. Men are scared, and they don't even come over to talk to me anymore. They're too afraid." So you do. You go talk to that man, you smile, you flirt, but you start asking him certain questions; questions that allow you to define his personality, questions that give him the unconscious feeling that you are sizing him up, just the way nature wants it to happen. He might feel as if he has to prove that he's worthy of you. Because of that, the attraction really starts to grow. You are already very interested in him, you've picked him, but you don't show this to him. You don't make it easy. You just walked up to him to break the ice. You make him work for it. By the end of the conversation, it's not you who asks his number. It's not even you who asks, "Can I see you again? Will I see you again?" No, you wait for him to ask it because you understand *he* has to pick you as well. If he doesn't, so be it. It wasn't meant to be.

If you play the game of love like this, you'll see that you will have a lot more success and waste less time with guys who weren't ready for you. You'll be practicing that very important thing called self-control as well. Even though you really want him, if *he* doesn't ask for your number or "can I see you again," you walk away. The right type of guy will step up, and that's the entire idea behind this book. The men who are naturally interested in you will step up, because of your newfound behavior, the little changes that you will implement in your life. They will make themselves known by picking you, by asking you out, and if you choose one of those guys, you won't walk up to that invisible wall if you keep playing your cards right. You won't be in a situation where "he doesn't know where this is going." Do you see the difference? This book is not about seducing every man and having a great relationship with any man you choose. This book is about selecting the right type of man and how to nurture that relationship so you can have an emotionally stable relationship with him. If you pick the guy who is willing to work for you and wants to prove himself to you, then that's the right type of man.

Imagine that you have a job interview. The guy who is taking the interview and asking you the questions is a 45-year-old man. He's tall. He has dark hair, a little moustache, and a serious face. You're sitting right in front of him. He says something like, "Would you like to come and work for us? This is what we have to offer. I hope that's enough for you. We really would like to have a long-term relationship with you, and we hope you can stay with us for a very long time." Does this guy already want you to come and work for him, or do you have to prove yourself to this type of guy? Is this guy still deciding whether or not he wants you or another candidate? Will you still feel "attracted" to this job opening?

Let's say you meet the same guy. You're sitting right in front of him. He says, "Why would you like to work here? What do you know about the company? Your resume says that you're very good at doing XYZ, what have you been doing with that?" After you answer his questions, he tells you, "Someone will call you and you will hear if you're selected or not by the end of the week." Does this guy want you to work for him? Do you feel the difference? What will make your more excited? Which of these two examples will make you think about the interview you had with this guy?

Try to imagine that you've just been in both situations here. Are you going to be eagerly waiting by the phone after the first job interview? Will you wonder, "Will they call? Yes or no?" For the second scenario where he asked all those questions, are you then going to be excited and waiting by the phone? Will you wonder, "Is he going to call or not to give me the job?" If you then get the job in the first example, are you going to be thinking, "Yes! I got the job!" If you then get the job in the second example, are you going to be thinking, "Yes! I got the job!" Do you feel the difference? I'm pretty sure that you will be a lot more excited in the second scenario, and we're talking about the exact same job offer here, but the interview process was different. In the first one, he shows he's *very* interested. He says, "Oh, I want you! You are the princess we are looking for, the solution to all of our problems." In the second one, he didn't make it that easy.

If you play this game with a man, if in the beginning you already say, "You're so handsome, and I'm so glad you asked me out. I could have never dreamt of being on a date with a guy like you." And yes, I'm exaggerating here, but if you give him those signals, he's not going to be excited. There's no excitement or challenge for him; there's no attraction. He's not going to think, "Is she going to call me? When I call her, is she going to pick up?"

When you make it a little bit more difficult (you still have to be sweet; you still have to help him), but if he thinks afterwards, "This is exciting. I think she likes me, but I'm not sure") then you will create the emotional attraction that will draw him in. Make him work for it; make him fight for you. You deserve a man who does. That's what men are supposed to do! Don't make it too easy. Don't make it too hard either.

If there's only one thing that you remember after this entire book, please let it be this: make him "work" for you. Make sure the insecurity or challenge is there. You don't have to behave like a diva, but make sure you add a zest of challenge and mystery and that you keep your self-control alive. If he feels on a subconscious level that the selection procedure is starting, that he has to prove to you that he's worthy of you, that he has to be better than the other men you could chose—*if* he already picked you out first and thus likes you—then he is going to feel that gut level attraction for you. That's something that works for every guy. He has to like you at least a bit, but what you do after will create that true and lasting attraction . . . or not.

The second most important thing you should remember is that you always get the man you choose. So if you follow the natural selection process where he picked you, you chose him by allowing him to take you out, and you feel that he's not really what you're looking for, don't try to change him. Simply dump him and go look for another man who has shown interest in you and has picked you as well. Choose that guy. Some women like a guy so much they think they'll be able to change him and take his flaws away. Trust me, you can't change anyone; his natural 'way' will always come back.

I truly hope I've shocked you here and there. That's when change happens. I hope you'll try to test my theories on the men you know or meet. I hope you will have an open mind and don't discard any of my theories before you've actually tested them yourself. You'll be surprised of the positive results you'll get.

It was a pleasure writing this book and I hope it brought you the insights you were looking for.

Good luck on the dating battlefield! And don't forget to join me on http://www.keephimattracted.com for free podcasts and newsletters with tips about men.

24065167R00063

Made in the USA
Lexington, KY
03 July 2013